STUDIES IN AFRICAN AMERICAN HISTORY AND CULTURE

edited by
GRAHAM HODGES
COLGATE UNIVERSITY

A GARLAND SERIES

PARALLEL COMMUNITIES

African Americans in California's East Bay 1850–1963

DELORES NASON McBROOME

GARLAND PUBLISHING, INC.
NEW YORK & LONDON / 1993

Copyright © 1993 Delores Nason McBroome
All rights reserved

Library of Congress Cataloging-in-Publication Data

McBroome, Delores Nason, 1948–
    Parallel communities : African Americans in California's East Bay, 1850–1963 / Delores Nason McBroome.
    p.   cm. — (Studies in African American history and culture)
    Includes bibliographical references and index.
    ISBN 0-8153-1462-0 (alk. paper)
    1. Afro-Americans—California—San Francisco Bay Area—History.
2. Afro-Americans—California—San Francisco Bay Area—Economic conditions. 3. San Francisco Bay Area (Calif.)—History. 4. San Francisco Bay Area (Calif.)—Economic conditions. I. Title. II. Series.
F868.S156M35   1993
979.4'600496073—dc20   93-8291
                                                                      CIP

Printed on acid-free, 250-year-life paper
Manufactured in the United States of America

For

my parents, Harold and Jean Nason

and my husband, William McBroome

Table of Contents

THE PROMISE AND REALITY OF THE CALIFORNIA
    DREAM 3

BUILDING COMMUNITY AND ECONOMIC
    INDEPENDENCE, 1900-1919 31

ECONOMIC MILITANCY CONFRONTS THE
    DICHOTOMY OF THE CALIFORNIA DREAM,
    1920-1939 55

CATALYST FOR CHANGE: WARTIME IN
    CALIFORNIA'S EAST BAY 91

THE STRUGGLE FOR LEGITIMACY, 1945-1963 129

EPILOGUE 151

BIBLIOGRAPHY 157

INDEX 181

Preface

Between 1850 and 1963 African-Americans in California's East Bay cities of Alameda, Berkeley, Oakland, and Richmond developed institutions that parallelled the dominant white societies residing in these same cities. However, the purpose of the African-American institutions differed from that of the neighboring white institutions. In addition to civic growth and prosperity, African-Americans sought to fulfill their own California Dreams of equality by building economic, political, and social institutions providing legitimacy for themselves and their children. Thus California's nineteenth-century African-Americans worked towards ending de facto discrimination in the state. They believed the promise of the California Dream would afford both the state's white and black residents a common ground where social dignity and economic ability for all people would be respected. This dream proved elusive during California's first century of statehood, and African-Americans began to develop their own institutions within their communities, parallel to the West's egalitarian creed but rarely sharing common ground with white Californians.

Nineteenth century African-Americans in California's East Bay fought strongly for their political freedom. Statewide colored conventions and the black press helped to petition the California legislature to extend the political rights of California's African-Americans during the 1850s and 1860s. Programs of African-American organizations and black churches sought political and social legitimacy for their East Bay communities. During the period from 1900 to 1930 these African-American programs became increasingly aware of the need to establish economic legitimacy for their members as well. Unemployment in the Great Depression triggered economic campaigns protesting labor discrimination against African-Americans. World War II and heavy wartime migration to California's defense industries served as catalysts encouraging opposition to segregation. African-American political and social organizations already in place by 1940 helped direct black communities lobbying for fair employment and housing practices after the Second World War. As postwar civil rights mobilization grew, African-Americans in the East Bay realized some legislative victories. Ironically this proved an important juncture as blacks found the California Dream slipping from their grasp. Although California's courts upheld Rumford's Fair Housing Act of 1963, California's voters had opposed it by a two-to-one ratio. Legislative campaigns opened many avenues for African-American advancement but failed to achieve the realization of a California Dream wherein black and white communities became one. Despite the efficacy of African-American institutions to provide legitimacy for their communities, black and white Californians remained divided by de facto discrimination in 1963. This book examines the nature of California's parallel communities in the East Bay and evaluates the African-American quest for legitimacy from 1850 to 1963.

Parallel Communities

CHAPTER I

THE PROMISE AND REALITY OF THE CALIFORNIA DREAM

African-Americans migrating to California in the mid-nineteenth century experienced much of the discrimination which existed elsewhere in the Union; however, they soon began to develop both political and social strategies to eliminate prejudice against them. The communities which they built reflected their aspirations and conviction that California would offer them freedom and opportunity. These desires were nurtured in an arid atmosphere of economic and social discrimination enforced by political proscriptions. African-Americans encountered at best a self-serving tolerance for economic endeavors or worse, hostilitity towards their physical presence in California, often surfacing in restrictions placed upon them by a predominant white population. These impediments refuted the egalitarian creed which the American West purported to observe. The aspirations of African-Americans often conflicted with the Golden State's reality expressed by the San Francisco *Californian* in 1849: "We desire only a white population in California."[1]

Yet this illusion of a white El Dorado had been breached as early as the sixteenth century when the Spanish navy carrying free blacks and slaves explored Mexico and California. Black men and women became an integral part of the Indian and Spanish population of the West. Settling California with the Franciscans in the eighteenth century these people of mixed ancestry became the first settlers of El Dorado. Estimates indicate that twenty percent of Spanish settlers in Baja California were of African ancestry by the eighteenth century.[2]

Perhaps it is fitting that the first permanent American residents of California should be two seamen—one black and one white—who saw California as a land of liberation and opportunity. In 1816 an African-American named Bob and a white sailor named

Thomas Doak left their ship, the *Albatross*, to become citizens of Spanish California. In 1819 Father Ripoll of the Santa Barbara mission baptized Bob who took the name Juan Cristobal while Thomas Doak became Felipe Santiago.[3] They found not only liberation from adversities of the sea but also from social contempt which early Americans held for the seagoing Jack Tars. California provided Juan Cristobal with an opportunity to gain acceptance in a new land untainted by racial disparity. The united action of Juan Cristobal and Felipe Santiago symbolized the California dream for African-Americans. It emphasized common ground where social dignity and economic abilities for all men, regardless of color, would be recognized. The Third Annual Convention for the Improvement of Free People of Color which met in Philadelphia in 1833 urged that:

> those who may be obliged to exchange a cultivated region for a howling wilderness, we recommend, to retire into the western wilds, and fell the native forest of America, where the ploughshare of prejudice has as yet been unable to penetrate the soil.[4]

This belief in the innocence of the American West would quickly be disproved by California settlers. Before California's constitutional convention of 1849, mass meetings discussed excluding "free persons of color" and quickly set a tone of racial disparity toward them. Edward Gilbert, a delegate to the convention, argued that the exclusion article was unfair as it had no provision to exclude:

> the miserable natives [from] the Sandwich Islands and the other Islands of the Pacific [or] the degraded wretches of Sidney, New South Wales, or the population of Chili, Peru, or Mexico.[5]

These people, Gilbert said, would pollute California's soil just as badly as the African-Americans. The resolution for exclusion failed to pass by a vote of 31 to 8.

Many of the mining districts resolved that any candidate to the state constitutional convention must be opposed to the extension of slavery in California. Although slavery was not permitted in the new state, abolitionist sentiment did not pervade the reasoning of the legislators. The threat which slave labor could pose in the mines motivated the delegates to the constitutional convention to outlaw slavery.[6] The Gold Rush quickened growth of the African-American population so that by 1850 over a thousand English and Spanish-speaking blacks were in California. The number of free black miners along a section of the American River was so large that the area was referred to as "Nigger Bar."[7] The majority of African-Americans in California were free men although some slaves were brought by Southern masters to work the mines. Since miners in California considered black or Indian labor unfair competition, Southerners mined with their slaves in isolated areas or resorted to a ruse pretending that their slaves owned the mines.[8] Popular lore led white miners to believe the African-American was especially lucky in discovering gold. By December 1848 the large free black communities of New York City and New Bedford, Massachusetts, read an article in their newspapers claiming that a black gold miner in California displayed a sack of gold dust valued at more than a hundred dollars which he claimed represented a day's pickings. The following month an army officer stationed in California wrote a letter reprinted in New York's *Albany Argus* which stated: "The merest Negro could make more than our present governor." In 1850 the *Liberator* published a letter signed by thirty-seven African-Americans who claimed to be earning between one hundred and three hundred dollars a month in California's mines.[9] These reports encouraged free blacks in the East to try their luck in California's Gold Rush. New York merchants paid for travel expenses and outfitted free blacks who would prospect for them in California. Even white Southerners succumbed to this belief. Eugene Berwanger's study, *The Frontier Against Slavery*, recounts the story of a Tennessee slave master, Thomas Gilman, allowing one of his slaves to go to California if the slave agreed to purchase his freedom with the gold he found in El Dorado. The African-American's image of El Dorado as a new frontier remained somewhat tarnished, however, as reports of racism in the western free states of Ohio, Indiana, and Illinois were confirmed. Many people believed that California would be open to slavery. Free black miners were often harassed from their claims during the Gold Rush years. J.D. Borthwick, an English traveller to California, recorded in 1851:

> In the mines the Americans seemed to exhibit more tolerance of Negro blood than usual in the states—not that Negroes were allowed to sit at tables with white men or considered to be all on an equality, but, owing partly to the exigencies of the unsettled states of society . . . Negroes were permitted to lose their money in the gambling rooms.[10]

Nevertheless, by 1852 California's African-American population had doubled within three years to form one-percent of the state's population (over 2000 people). Most African-Americans turned from mining claims to seeking employment as waiters, barbers, and general laborers in the new state. Reports filtered back to eastern residents that Negro cooks were in demand in California and could earn as much as $125 a month.[11] Others went into business for themselves. Mary Ellen ("Mammy") Pleasant came to San Francisco as a forty-niner after inheriting $50,000 from her late husband's estate. She used this money to open a boardinghouse where she issued loans at high interest rates and speculated in real estate property. Like other black Californians, Mammy Pleasant devoted herself to the abolition cause by using her money to aid runaway slaves. She is alleged to have travelled to Chatham, Canada, in 1858 in order to give John Brown $30,000 to help him incite his slave rebellion at Harper's Ferry.[12]

The dreams of African-Americans and white settlers in California, however, often differed. Peter Burnett, as first Governor of California in the temporary capital at San Jose, desired to establish a California community which would be superior to those in the East; however, he believed this could only happen if California "avoided the evils . . . of mixed races." When John McDougal succeeded Peter Burnett as California's Governor in 1850 he refused to pardon any African-American serving sentences in the state prison. He believed, like Burnett, that the African-Americans were unworthy of citizenship because they were noted for intoxication and laziness.[13] Excluded from suffrage and state militia service, African-Americans developed separate communities patterned after white society. Although creating their own newspapers, political and fraternal clubs, and schools, California's black community remained cognizant of their need to legitimize or "justify their inclusion in the general society."[14] This struggle for legitimacy began with their exclusion from suffrage and the right to give testimony in court. The constitutional convention limited suffrage to white males. The new state on 16 April 1850 passed Section 14 of California's Criminal Practices Act. This disqualified "Negroes, Mulattoes and persons having one-eighth Negro blood from giving testimony where a white person is a party." The following year, Section 394 of the Civil Practices Act disqualified "colored persons from giving testimony in civil cases where a white is involved."[15] When the murderer of Gordon Chase, a Negro barber in San Francisco, was allowed to go free although an eyewitness was present, the right to testimony became a crucial issue to African-Americans. The witness, a man named Robert Cowles, was not allowed to testify because a "corps of physicians . . . decided that his hair showed he had one-sixteenth part of a drop of Negro blood."[16] Several prominent black leaders organized the Franchise League with abrogation of proscriptive black laws as its main objective.

Dissatisfaction with the new state laws caused some thirty-five African-American settlers in California to migrate to British Columbia after they watched in frustration as the state courts dealt with the Archy Lee case. C.A. Stovall of Mississippi brought his slave, Archy Lee, with him to Sacramento where he stayed for five months managing a cattle ranch, teaching school and hiring out his slave and eventually selling him to Robert Blakely. When Lee escaped from Blakely, he was first ruled free by the U.S. Commissioner for California, George Johnston, whose ruling was upheld by a Sacramento County court. Later Stovall apprehended his former slave and claimed he was only passing through California and stayed in Sacramento to recover his health. When the case reached the State Supreme Court in 1858, Chief Justice Peter Burnett found:

> that the master had forfeited his right to the slave by bringing him to a free state after its admission to the Union and by remaining for a substantial time, but ruled that an exception should be made because the master was young, in poor health, and in need of his slave's services.[17]

This decision so disillusioned many African-Americans in California that several free blacks brought up the suggestion that they emigrate to Vancouver Island, Sonora, or to New Granada in Panama. Even the final release of Archy Lee did not quell their anger. Although California's black leaders were "thumpingly against colonization and emigration," a group of thirty-five African-Americans (including Archy Lee) steamed out of San Francisco Bay on April 22, 1858 aboard the *Commodore* hoping to find liberty in the gold rush at Fraser River in British Columbia.[18] Approximately 400 African-Americans from California followed these first settlers over the next two years. The Executive Committee of the Colored People of the State of California noted in 1859 that:

> in the late great Fraser excitement, when the desire to migrate to the new El Dorado became a mania, pervading all classes, many of our best men, the bone and sinew, the wealth and intelligence of our people, became infatuated with the golden prospects, and left the State for a new theatre of action.[19]

Even the optimism of the Executive Committee waned after the migrations took place, for it would not meet again until 1864.

Equal education, suffrage, use of public facilities and accommodations, vocational limitation, and residential mobility were all denied to the African-American in California. Public meetings protesting these proscriptive laws as well as a petition drive in San Francisco were ignored by white Californians. Fearful that they were being locked into the racial prejudices of Easterners, blacks in California called for a statewide convention of colored citizens in 1855. Promoted by black ministers the convention took place at the colored Methodist Church in Sacramento on November 20, 1855. The delegates met:

> for the purpose of taking into consideration the propriety of petitioning the Legislature of California, for a change in the law relating to the testimony of colored people in the courts of justice in this State. Also to adopt plans for the general improvement of their condition throughout the State.[20]

William H. Yates of San Francisco became the permanent chairman of the State Convention of Colored Citizens first organized in 1855. This convention set up an Executive Committee of ten people from San Francisco, Sacramento, and Marysville. The lobbying efforts of this committee were of paramount concern to the delegates as many of them, like Yates, were abolitionists and sought to free California from proscriptive laws as well as the Fugitive Slave Law of 1852.[21] One of their first actions at the 1855 convention approved a circular issued in the name of the First State Convention of the Colored Citizens of the State of California which petitioned the legislature and made resolutions regarding the repeal of the prohibitive laws against African-Americans.[22] In 1856 over 700 people from San Francisco alone signed these petitions which were presented to the California Senate where they were officially received. The petitions were then sent to the judiciary committee where they were scuttled.

The State Convention of Colored Citizens of 1856 was held again in Sacramento. On the third day of the convention, the Committee on a State Press encouraged the convention to support a statewide newspaper, the *Mirror of the Times*. This weekly newspaper already established in San Francisco became the official organ of the State Convention. The Committee urged that its oversized format be reduced to one-fourth its present size and that it be supported by a General Fund of colored citizens in California.[23] The commitment of the convention delegates for an African-American press in California remained strong although the *Mirror of the Times* would be short-lived. The State Executive Committee exhorted delegates from all California counties to come to the financial aid of the *Mirror*. Its efforts failed; yet, the Committee clearly indicated its belief that an African-American press was essential to California's promise. The 1859 *Address of the State Executive Committee to the Colored People of the State of California* called the *Mirror* "the great mouthpiece of the people" and judged the majority of counties "criminally remiss in not furnishing their support."[24] William Henry Yates recognized the need for a free press which could disseminate legislative proposals. Yates became a member of the publishing committee for the San Francisco *Elevator*, a newspaper that wrote "Equality Before the Law" under its masthead.[25] By the late 1860s there would be two African-American newspapers published in the Bay Area—the San Francisco *Pacific Appeal* and the San Francisco *Elevator*.[26] Although the son of a free man, Yates was born in the District of Columbia to a slave mother. Having purchased his own freedom for the sum of $1000 by working as custodian at the U.S. Supreme Court and running his own business, Yates valued the liberty which the California Dream promised. Leaving Washington, D.C., after

1845 under a cloud of suspicion that he had aided fugitive slaves, Yates went to New York where he became a steward of the Manhattan Club. After losing his money in a restaurant venture with a "faithless" partner, he took the steamship *Golden Gate* to San Francisco in 1851 where he worked for the California Steam Navigation Company. Yates exemplifies the aspirations of African-Americans in California, for he made repeal of black laws his goal from 1852 until they were revoked in 1862.[27]

Repeal of the antagonistic laws became known as the "right to testimony" struggle. This claim merged with the promise of the California Dream to encourage African-Americans in their struggle for legitimacy:

> Now, we answer [to the question why colored men are not satisfied in California] that we are men, and Americans—free men; born on the soil; and claim all the rights and immunities that any other class of men enjoy, not by adoption, but by right of birth.
> If we own houses, ranches, stores, mining claims, and barber shops, or any other property, we are taxed for it in common with others, to support the Government, and be protected in the peaceful enjoyment of our just earnings.[28]

The Executive Committee was tireless in its efforts to redress the wrongs it saw in the Golden State. In 1856 it convened four times throughout the year: three times in Sacramento and once in Marysville. It continued to push for repeal of the discriminatory laws. The committee met again in 1857 to resolve that African-Americans had the "right to testimony" and the moral abilities to expect equal protection from equal taxation. The resolutions protested that California's "black laws" made crimes against the African-American easy. The Committee protested a decision by the United States Land Office that said Negroes could not preempt claims to public lands. It was a decision which the *Pacific Appeal* called a "fitting successor to the . . . Taney Decision." Homestead laws for California were passed in 1851 and 1860. Section Two of the 1851 law exluded Negroes by its statement:

> Whenever any white man or female resident in this State shall desire to avail himself or herself of the benefits of this act,

such person shall make a written application to the county judge of the county in which the land is situated.

In 1860 another resolution passed the California Legislature which resolved that Congressmen:

> use their influence to procure the passage of a law by Congress donating to each bona fide settler on the public agricultural lands within the State, being a free white person over the age of twenty-one years and a citizens of the United States; who shall have become such a homestead community of one hundred and sixty acres or more after a continuous residence and occupation thereof for five years.[29]

Because African-Americans could theoretically buy a home or property (and some did), the right to testimony if their claim was challenged in court by a white person was essential to their wellbeing. The "homestead question" and the "right to testimony" were considered important first steps to "ameliorate the condition of America's colored sons and daughters."[30]

Through the combined efforts of the State Executive Committee, the African-American churches and newspapers lobbying to restore "right to testimony" remained in the forefront of early California's political concerns. It is through these agencies that the struggle for African-American legitimacy in California took shape. For example, in its address of 1859, the State Executive Committee reported:

> There are those of our own race who are endued [sic] with powers to enter any vocation through the instrumentality of which other men obtain wealth and distinction. To that favored class of our people, the incipient work of our elevation should be entrusted. Pecuniary prominence, in a country so diversified as this, takes precedence over intellectual, and it should be our highest aim to seek the end we have marked out, through that mode which has formed a superiority, and left many of us far behind the business progress of the age. The broad expanse of agriculture, commerce, mining, and mechanism invites mind and energy to the enjoyment of its rewards and the preferment it confers.[31]

There were several men in the Bay Area by 1862 who saw political rights as essential to the growth of any African-American community in California. The Reverend John J. Moore of San Francisco's African Methodist Episcopal (hereafter A.M.E.) Zion Church wrote a statement for the *Lunar Visitor* that indicated African-American goals in California:

1. We want *unity of sympathy* . . .
2. We want *unity of purpose* . . .
3. We want *unity of particular interest* in our own race . . .
4. We want *unity of confidence* in ourselves . . .
5. We want the *unity of self-respect* . . . [32]

In its first issue on Saturday, 4 April 1862, the *Pacific Appeal's* editor Phillip A. Bell proclaimed the *Appeal* to:

> be devoted to the interests of the Colored people of California and to their Moral, Intellectual and Political advancement. . . . We have nothing to disguise; we enter the field boldly, fearlessly, but with dignity and calmness to appeal for the rights of the Colored Citizens of this State.[33]

Joined by the *Morning Call*, the *Herald and Mirror*, the *Bulletin*, and the *Alta*, the *Pacific Appeal* continued to call for a right to testimony bill throughout the spring and summer of 1862. All the papers except the *Evening Journal* supported a petition circulating throughout the San Francisco Bay area to permit African-Americans the right to testimony. Although the California Assembly passed the bill by a majority, the Senate refused it by a 15 to 13 vote in early 1862. While the *Morning Call* saw the failure to repeal the black laws as a mistake, the *Evening Journal* praised the Senate.[34] It was obvious that better organization was needed to urge the repeal of laws restricting right to testimony.

By fall 1862, the Negro Testimony Bill (Perkins Bill) became a bellwether for African-American support of legislators. Although African-Americans could not exercise suffrage in California, a careful count was maintained by the *Pacific Appeal* of all members of the legislature who voted for and against the bill. Satisfaction was noted when all members who voted affirmatively on the Negro Testimony Bill were reelected; while most legislators who voted against the bill were not nominated or defeated in their bids for reelection. In early 1863 Bill No. 2 (re: civil cases) and Bill No. 3 (re: right to testimony in criminal cases) passed the Assembly 21 to 14 and 22 to 15 respectively.[35] All San Francisco area representatives voted for the right to testimony which indicates the strength of the petition drives and news campaigns in the Bay Area. In March 1863, Phillip A. Bell met with Governor Leland Stanford to urge his endorsement of the bills. Stanford informed Bell that he had signed the Testimony Bills thereby lifting one of the hurdles which African-Americans experienced in their quest for liberation and opportunity in California.[36] Also in 1863 a U.S. Land Commissioner found in favor of blacks holding title to property which resolved the Homestead issue.

Simultaneously with their victory over the testimony bills, African-Americans in the San Francisco Bay area began to discuss the poor condition of black public schools. The *Pacific Appeal* reported fifty students crowded in a badly ventilated basement in San Francisco. A petition was presented to the School Board with little redress offered.[37] Oakland's first private school for black children opened in 1857 under the direction of Elizabeth Thorn-Scott. When she died ten years later, her school closed and a one-room public school for black children opened at Tenth Avenue and East Eleventh Street in the township of Brooklyn with Mary Sanderson as its teacher.[38] Mrs. Stewart opened a private school for infants and toddlers in 1863; while an evening school for adults was opened by the Reverend J.B. Sanderson in 1867.[39]

By 1868 the *Morning Call* was engaged in a debate with the editor of the *Elevator* over the legality of public schools for African-American children. The *Morning Call* claimed that: "Negroes are not entitled by law to have sufficient schools for the accommodation of their children maintained at the public expense." Phillip A. Bell's editorials took the *Call* to task for its "attempts to justify the Board of Education for closing the colored school on Broadway before selecting any other place for the education of our children."[40] General Cobb, the City Director of Public Schools in San Francisco, ordered the Broadway Colored School to close because it was contiguous to a white school and a nuisance to white children.[41] Editor Bell of the San Francisco *Elevator* charged General Cobb in several editorials:

> with malignant and persistent opposition to our school because of our color. Ever since he has been in the Board he has endeavored to have that school broken up. He first pronounced it a nuisance; now he says the black children behave worse than the white children. How consistent! He has achieved his object and he need not be surprised if we are indignant.[42]

Bell, a long-time abolitionist, particularly disliked Cobb's background as a slave trader in Galveston, Texas, and claimed that "He still retains the brutal instincts of his former degrading business."[43]

The issue of exclusion of African-American children from public school services captured the attention of most Californians in the late 1860s due to the heavy immigration of Chinese into the state. By 1860, while there were approximately 4,086 African-Americans in California, there were 34,933 Chinese in the state. African-American editors soon found themselves defending the right of black children to attend public schools on the basis of Americanism. In 1867, Bell elucidates this position in his editorials:

> The Negro is a native American, loyal to the government, and a lover of his country and her institutions—American in all his ideas; a Christian by education, and a believer of the truths of Christianity from principle. The Chinese are foreigners, unacquainted with our system of government, adhering to their own habits and customs, and of heathen or idolatrous faith.[44]

In other words Bell led his readers to believe that the Chinese in California did not try to assimilate into California's society whereas African-Americans deserved civil rights by virtue of their adherence to American institutions. Anti-Chinese sentiment grew strong in California as jobs became scarce after 1860. Patricia Nelson Limerick captures this economic drive towards Chinese exclusion in *The Legacy of Conquest* when she states:

> To white workingmen, post-gold rush California did not live up to its promise. Facing limited job opportunities and uncertain futures, white laborers looked both for solutions and for scapegoats. Men in California came with high hopes; jobs proved scarce and unrewarding; someone must be to blame.

In California, capital had at its command a source of controllable, underpaid labor. White workers, the historian Alexander Saxton has said, "viewed the Chinese as tools of monopoly."[45] African-Americans faced the closing of the Brooklyn public school for black children in 1871. Presented with arguments for greater African-American assimilation into white society, the small township of Brooklyn reconsidered its position later that year and decided to allow black children living within its jurisdiction access to the town's public school provided for white children; however, it would not permit black children from Oakland to attend. Without public school opportunities for black children in Oakland, the city's Board of Education voted five to two in favor of admitting eight "children of African descent" to any of Oakland's public schools in May, 1872.[46]

The State Convention of Colored Citizens of the State of California held in 1873 called attention to the state's segregated public schools and held the Republican party responsible for the failure of African-Americans to gain political representation in the state. As early as 1874 Phillip A. Bell led a revolt from African-American support for the Republicans when he founded the Equal Rights League which would support the Democratic ticket in 1877.[47] Now political and community response to discrimination coalesced in church-sponsored programs. First established in 1858 as a mission, Oakland's black residents took turns hosting church meetings in their homes until 1863 when a building and minister were secured to form the Shiloh African Methodist Episcopal Church at Seventh and Market Streets. It seemed only natural that the Shiloh A.M.E. Church in Oakland would become the meeting place for Oakland citizens concerned about the state's educational direction; the church building originally served as Oakland's first schoolhouse before it was moved to its A.M.E. location.[48] Oakland's black residents used the church site for meetings endorsing a statewide black educational conference held in Stockton in 1871 to urge an end to segregated schools. Its action was repeated by several African-American communities and recognized by legislators in the Capitol. The Stockton convention agreed to hire John W. Dwinelle to represent their case before the state Supreme Court. His arguments, based on the Thirteenth and Fourteenth Amendments and the Civil Rights Act of 1866, stated that separate schools create "an odious distinction of caste." Dwinelle kept the case before the court for two years while the justices delayed their decision due to the case's controversial nature. The Court's decision did not support Dwinelle's argument but agreed that racism might be diminished through integrated schools. The justices agreed that where no separate schools for black children existed they must be admitted to white schools.[49] This decision did not address the cases of African-American children who desired to attend white schools because they were closer to their homes than the black schools in their areas. As a result Senator Finney introduced a new school bill in early 1872 which asked the Legislature to modify the school laws as to permit colored children the same common school privileges as white children.[50] In 1880 the California Legislature eliminated from all state laws references to separate schools for black children. This was reinforced in 1890 when the State Supreme Court declared in *Wysinger vs. Crookshank* that "separate schools cannot be established for colored children."[51]

These bills passed partly as a result of the factionalism existing within California's political parties. The Democratic party had experienced its own splinter group with the formation of the Union-Democratic ticket in 1867. Most Californians had come to support the Union by the end of the Civil War and wished to bolt from the pro-southern leadership of the regular Democrats. Thus the Union party drew both those Democrats who wished to ally with the railroad interests in running their communities (the "Short Hairs") and the Republican Unionists (the "Long Hairs") who although supportive of the transcontinental railroad venture were cautious about subsidizing the Central Pacific with taxpayer's monies.[52] Opponents of the Union Party soon were claiming that its leaders supported a "Mongrel party" and quite flagrantly opposed racial equality. The San Francisco *Examiner* claimed Unionists were:

> for a white man's government, constitutionally administered, against a great Mongrel military despotism, upheld by a union of the purse and the sword, and sought to be perpetuated through negro and Chinese votes.[53]

The *Examiner's* vitriolic diatribes against Chinese and Negro immigrants pushed the Long Hairs as well as Republicans to oppose the bigotry of the regular Democrats. Unwilling to accept an end to Chinese immigration because the completion of the railroad and the draining and irrigation of California farmlands depended upon Chinese cheap labor, the *Examiner's* opponents focused instead upon the Negro's right to fair opportunity. The California *Alta* took the Republican and Long Hair position when it stated:

> We cannot force public opinion; but at least until that manifests a disposition to give the Negro a fair and equal chance, let us not draw unfair and unjust comparisons, holding the black man up as a moral reprobate, whose vices are all his own and whose virtues are to be credited to our example. The reverse of this boast is much nearer the truth.[54]

Desire for Chinese exclusion diverted attention from African-American activities in California even before the Civil War. Edward E. France noted in his 1962 study of the migration of the Negro to the San Francisco Bay area that:

> Perhaps the agitation against the Chinese at this time [1858] saved the Negroes from further harassment until the events succeeding the Civil War solved the questions of citizenship, suffrage, and to a smaller degree certain other civil rights.[55]

It is against this backdrop that African-Americans barely escaped the exclusion practices which befell the Chinese immigrant to California.

All three of the Reconstruction Amendments offered California's African-American settlers political voice and new hope for an egalitarian community. The Thirteenth Amendment by abolishing slavery eliminated the fear of reprisal under the Fugitive Slave Law. Although liable for prosecution, the majority of African-Americans in California before the Civil War were brazenly abolitionist in their stance. In 1859 two slaves—Peter and Hannah Wilson—were brought by the Byrne family to Berkeley only to be forcibly rescued from bondage by a group of black abolitionists from Oakland.[56] California ratified the Thirteenth Amendment to the U.S. Constitution without opposition; however, the other Reconstruction amendments would not fare as well. Because the Fourteenth Amendment guaranteed citizenship rights and equal protection of the law to all native-born Americans there was a great deal of reluctance throughout the state in ratifying such a law. Since the statewide Colored Convention of 1865 endorsed black suffrage as well as a constitutional amendment which would change California's voting regulations, many voters saw the Fourteenth Amendment as an attempt to introduce racial factionalism in the state's politics. When the Fifteenth Amendment extended voting rights to all male citizens, California voters rejected it. Addressing the Democratic convention in Sacramento in 1869 Governor Henry H. Haight discouraged ratification of the Fifteenth Amendment because of its implied threat to states' rights and inclusion of Chinese suffrage. Haight did not care:

> ... whether the motive is to seek to perpetuate political power and official emoluments by the aid of negro and Chinese suffrage, or whether it is to gratify feelings of ill will against the seceded and border slave states—whether it is to form a profitable alliance between wealthy corporations and purchasable voters or whether it is crack-brained humanitarianism run mad.[57]

In 1870 Haight submitted the Fifteenth Amendment to the California Legislature and denounced it as unconstitutional. The grounds for Haight's argument rest on his belief that the amendment denied the states a reserved right—the right to set voting qualifications. Haight feared that:

> If this Amendment is adopted, the most degraded Digger Indian within our borders becomes at once an elector and, so far, a ruler. His vote would count for as much as that of the most intelligent white man in the State. In this event, also, by a slight amendment to the naturalization laws, the Chinese population could be made electors.[58]

Considering California's fear of losing its state rights to the federal government Edward E. France suggests that: "Possibly the failure to ratify the fifteenth amendment was meant as a rebuff to the national government rather than as an act of discrimination against the Negro."[59]

Although supportive of the Fifteenth Amendment, the Republican Party did not win the support of California's African-Americans. The statewide Colored Convention of 1873 encouraged a tendency among African-Americans to shy away from the

Republican party on the grounds that the party was not responsive to black political patronage. Civil service jobs were not given as political rewards to black voters although elsewhere in the nation during Reconstruction the Republican Party had awarded civil service positions to African-Americans. In 1874 Oakland leaders, Jeremiah B. Sanderson, Royall Lockett, and Z.J. Purnell founded a chapter of the Equal Rights League for the East Bay. It declared independence from the Republican Party and supported the Democratic ticket. In 1878 this Black Independent Club criticized those Republican officials who refused to appoint African-Americans to civil service jobs. The last statewide Colored Convention in 1882 would decide that supporting the Democratic Party would bring more political rewards for the African-American communities in the state. Finally in 1889 John Wilds became the first African-American on the Oakland civil service list when he was hired as janitor for the City Hall.[60]

Neither political party was favorable to the African-American vote after 1870 (the state of California did not ratify the Fifteenth Amendment until 1962). It quickly became apparent that political patronage would be essential to community growth. Beginning with San Francisco in 1891 most communities built African-American leagues in the late nineteenth century which represented community leaders' goals for economic opportunity and social dignity. The Leagues recognized the need to equate economic opportunity with political gains in order to win over those blacks who accepted Booker T. Washington's accommodationist doctrine rather than active political representation.[61] Their work was essential in building a strong African-American community within the state so that the political attitudes held by many within the Capital might change in response to pressure. In his annual message to the legislature, Governor Peter H. Burnett had said in 1851:

> Although it is assumed in the Declaration of Independence as a self-evident truth, that all men are born free and equal, it is equally true that there must be acquired as well as natural abilities to fit men for self-government. Without considering whether there be any reason for the opinion entertained by many learned persons that the colored races by nature are inferior to the white, and without attaching any importance to such opinions, still it may be safely affirmed that no race of men, under the precise

circumstances of this class in our state, could ever hope to advance to a single step in knowledge or virtue.[62]

According to Warren A. Beck and David A. Williams in their history of California, this attitude prevailed among the state's lawmakers.[63]

Yet, California's African-American community continued to trust in traditional political organization to gain social dignity and equality. During the Civil War with the black press their only advocate, pressure mounted for access to public transportation. San Francisco's *Pacific Appeal* editorialized against the ejection of two black women who boarded a streetcar after a funeral and were told to get off by the driver in the spring of 1863. William Bowen brought charges against a conductor of the City Railway Cars in San Francisco for forcibly ejecting him in May 1863.[64] Phillip A. Bell (not yet editor of the *Elevator*) wrote a letter to the San Francisco *Bulletin* in order to protest the policy of the Omnibus Railroad which contended that "passengers object to riding with black people. He believed that passengers would continue to use the railroad despite a few black people riding in a car." Bowen won his case and the judge fined the conductors who ejected William Bowen $25 each or ten days in jail.[65] In 1866 African-Americans won the right to ride San Francisco's streetcars in the case of *Brown vs. Omnibus Railroad Company*.[66] After being ejected from a horse-drawn streetcar, Charlotte Brown challenged the unwritten policy that Negroes could not use the streetcars. Her father successfully sued Omnibus Railroad for $5000 in damages.

Transportation, however, would remain central to the quest for legitimacy by the Bay Area's African-American community. Not only did it need to avail itself of easy access around the Bay but it also required jobs from the transportation companies. By 1869 Oakland became the western terminus for the Central Pacific Railroad. Coupled with the new sleeping cars for long distance travel introduced by the Pullman Company which hired only black porters, the Central Pacific Railroad emerged as a potential source of employment for African-Americans in the Bay Area. Since Oakland was the end of the line, it became home to many porters and railroad workers. Within the following decade Oakland grew from a population of 55 black residents to 593 (even Berkeley counted 11 African-Americans in its 1880 census). The new transcontinental railroad not only gave Oakland residents new opportunities for employment but also provided it with a sense of cosmopolitan pride. When Phillip Bell visited Oakland in May 1869 he indicated what many San Franciscans believed about the Contra Costa ("other coast") area:

> We visited this beautiful suburban city on Sunday last, and was [sic] agreeable surprised to witness the improvements in progress there. While we do not anticipate it will ever rival or equal this city, it will become, with increased ferry facilities to San Francisco, what Brooklyn is to New York.[67]

A regional identity came to life during these mid-nineteenth century decades. Social Darwinism came to pervade much of the fantastic doctrines put forth by California's early enthusiasts. Kevin Starr in *Americans and the California Dream, 1850-1915*, points out that beliefs in the physical attributes of Californians matching the state's healthy climate and bountiful harvests were not only based in eugenics but in a moral and aesthetic sense as well. Essayists, poets, and preachers spoke of their dreams in terms of a Mediterranean analogy:

> Here, they dreamed, might be an American people possessing fire and repose, amplitude and line, a healthy naturalism and a capacity for religion. Here might the American-as-Californian, the American-as-neo-Mediterranean, reach back behind his English-speaking heritage and possess himself of the spurned gifts of the South. 'Whatever Greece, Italy and Spain were in their noblest days, that we, also hope to become . . .,' Charles H. Shinn exhorted. 'A Cosmopolitan people, not narrow or prejudiced, strong, earnest, truthful, original; state-builders, home-lovers, believers in education, full of nature's naturalness-this is that end to which we of a ruder, more fertile age must toil, setting our faces toward the morning.'[68]

This dream for a Pacific Civilization caught fire among African-Americans on the other coast. Editors often alluded to the analogy when they wrote that Oakland was the Athens of the West. Just as San Francisco appropriated its claim to be the heir to the Roman Empire, Oakland and the East Bay identified with the democracy and progressive thought of the Greeks.

With the onset of a regional identity it became easier to build a sense of community pride. African-Americans in the East Bay established their communal identity through the black press and church. The power of the African-American press to instruct, persuade, and protest would remain constant throughout the nineteenth century. Likewise the church would provide similar opportunities as well as a meeting place—congregations serving their communities. Since Methodism was California's largest denomination in the nineteenth century, it is not surprising that Shiloh African Methodist Epicopal Church would be Oakland's first black congregation.[69] It provided the meeting hall for political and educational activities as well as the site for club and social functions. African-Americans who were not of the A.M.E. persuasion attended white churches in the area but were not allowed leadership roles. In 1889 the building of Beth Eden Baptist Church challenged the predominance of the African Methodist Episcopal church. Within the following decade three more churches came into existence: Ebenezer Baptist Church, New Hope Baptist Church, and Cooper A.M.E. Zion Church.[70] In 1892 the pastor of Beth Eden Baptist Church noted how Oakland's black community was a credit to its city:

> Surely no class of people have a better right to the cosmopolitan spirit of California than our "brother in black." We come not as foreigners but as American citizens. Those who, by the incidental circumstances to which they have been subjected, have stiffened the back bone of the Republic. They bring to the State such a reinforcement of industry, that some have styled them the best laborers in the world. . . . Oakland may be congratulated on an accession of citizens generally law abiding and self-reliant; for the Police Courts, alms-houses, etc., will show a more creditable record in favor of the colored people than any other class of citizens. Moreover, they are taxpayers of no little concern and good consumers. . . .[71]

The churches themselves relied upon the tireless work of their parishoners to raise the funds to keep afloat. The *Elevator* often advertised church affairs so that they might be well attended. The Ladies Ministerial Aid Society of Oakland held "pleasant socials in the lecture room of the First A.M.E. Church, 15th Street, every

Tuesday evening" to raise money to assist the Trustees and Stewards in paying for church expenses.[72]

In addition to the special community-building roles of the black press and church, black Masonry became an integral part of African-American life in California. The state's first Negro Masonic lodge was organized in San Francisco in 1854, and several other lodges were organized by the end of the decade.

In seeking legitimacy the African-American community created the legislative and communal associations which it saw as the operative centers of white society in California. However, it could not foresee the years of struggle and slow gain which these associations would encounter. Tainted by patterns of early discrimination, the dream of an egalitarian society in California faltered. In that misstep came the introduction of a parallel community to California's white society. The contrapuntal dreams of the two communities—black and white—competed with each other throughout the nineteenth and twentieth centuries. The African-American community sought legitimacy as its prize. This goal had been set as early as 1855 when William H. Newby said:

> We are an oppressed people, the subjects of a bitter prejudice, which we are now seeking to overcome. In appealing to our oppressors, we desire to do so in a manner that will have weight.[73]

The following chapters will suggest what strategies and limits to the success the East Bay's African-American community encountered in seeking legitimacy.

NOTES

1. *San Francisco Californian*, 5 March 1849, p. 1. For further discussion of the California Dream, see Kevin Starr, *Americans and the California Dream, 1850-1915* (New York: Oxford University Press, 1973). Patricia Nelson Limerick's book, *The Legacy of Conquest: The Unbroken Past of the American West* (W.W. Norton & Company, 1987) provides an intellectual framework for understanding how the concepts of conquest and legitimacy in the American West's past shape its present.

2. Rudolph M. Lapp, *Blacks in Gold Rush California* (New Haven and London: Yale University Press, 1977), 2. For further discussion of the mixed ancestry of the early California settlers, see Jack D. Forbes, "Black Pioneers: The Spanish-Speaking Afro-Americans of the Southwest," *Phylon* 27 (1966): 233-46; Douglas Henry Daniels, *Pioneer Urbanites: A Social and Cultural History of Black San Francisco* (Philadelphia: Temple University Press, 1980); Kenneth Wiggins Porter, *The Negro on the American Frontier* (New York: Arno Press, 1971); William Sherman Savage, *Blacks in the West* (Westport, Conn.: Greenwood Press, 1976).

3. Discrepancies exist as to whether the seamen were captured by Spaniards or jumped ship. H.H. Bancroft stated in his *History of the Pacific States of North America* that the men and their captain were captured; while Kevin Starr claims they jumped ship. Hubert Howe Bancroft, *History of the Pacific States of North America*, vol. 2, *California* (San Francisco: A.L. Bancroft & Co., 1885), 175. Starr, *Americans and the California Dream*, 12; Lapp, *Blacks in Gold Rush California*, 3.

4. Starr, *Americans and the California Dream*, 12; James A. Fisher, "The Political Development of the Black Community in California, 1850-1950," *California Historical Quarterly*, 50 (Sept. 1971): 257.

5. Eugene H. Berwanger, *The Frontier Against Slavery: Western Anti-Negro Prejudice and the Slavery Extension Controversy* (Urbana: University of Illinois, 1967), 68.

6. Malcolm Edwards, "The War of Complexional Distinction: Blacks in Gold Rush California & British Columbia," *California Historical Quarterly* 66 (Spring 1977): 36.

7. Although mining camps such as "Nigger Bar" gave onlookers the impression that large numbers of African-Americans were involved in mining, Eugene Berwanger's study of California shows

only one-third of the state's 962 African-Americans lived in mining districts in 1850. Berwanger, *The Frontier Against Slavery*, 60.

8. Velesta Jenkins, "White Racism and Black Response in California History," in *Ethnic Conflict in California History*, ed. Charles Wollenberg (Los Angeles: Tinnon-Brown, Inc., Book Publishers, 1970), 124. In the book, *Three Years in California* (1860), Walter Colton wrote that the miners were not concerned about "slavery in the abstract or as it exists in other communities; not one in ten cares a button for its abolition, nor the Wilmot Proviso either; all they look at is their own position; they must themselves swing the pick, and they won't swing it by the side of negro slaves." Berwanger, *The Frontier Against Slavery*, 61-62.

9. Lapp, *Blacks in Gold Rush California*, 12-13.

10. J.D. Borthwick, *Three Years in California* (London: 1857; reprint, Oakland, 1948), 134-135.

11. Lapp, *Blacks in Gold Rush California*, 22. The independence of Negro cooks is also noted in Leonard Kip, *California Sketches with Recollections of the Gold Mines* (Los Angeles, 1946), 51.

12. Kenneth G. Goode, *California's Black Pioneers: A Brief Historical Survey* (Santa Barbara, California: McNally & Loftin, Publishers, 1974), 87-88. Although flawed by inaccuracy, a biography on Mary Ellen Pleasant does exist: Helen Holdredge, *Mammy Pleasant* (New York: G.P. Putnam's Sons, 1953).

13. Berwanger cites Burnett as arguing that if Negroes were allowed to live in California without social and civil equality they would only be forced into a still further degraded nature. By 1857 the state prison director, James Estell, sent California's African-American inmates to New Orleans where they were sold into slavery. Berwanger, *The Frontier Against Slavery*, 70, 75.

14. Hardy Frye, "Negroes in California from 1841 to 1875," *California History Series*, vol. 3 (San Francisco: San Francisco Negro Historical and Cultural Society, 1968), 4.

15. Berwanger, *The Frontier Against Slavery*, 60-77; *The Pacific Appeal*, May 17, 1862, p. 2.

16. Frye, "Negroes in California from 1841 to 1875," 7.

17. Edwards, "The War of Complexional Distinction, 38; Berwanger, *The Frontier Against Slavery*, 71f.

18. Lapp points out that a large number of California's African-Americans came from New Bedford, Massachusetts, "which was a thoroughly anticolonization town" believing it would only serve as

a tool in the interests of slave-owners. Lapp, *Blacks in Gold Rush California*, 250. The date for the *Commodore's* departure has been reported as April 22 by Rudolph Lapp and as April 20 by Malcolm Edwards. See Lapp, *Blacks in Gold Rush California*, 242-243 and Edwards, "The War of Complexional Distinction, 41.

19. *Ibid.*, 41.

20. *Proceedings of the First State Convention of the Colored Citizens of the State of California, 1855* (Sacramento: Democratic State Journal Print, 1855; repr., 1969), 3.

21. A large number of the leaders of the statewide conventions subscribed to the *Frederick Douglass' Paper* which revealed their abolitionist sentiment. The black leadership's preference for Douglass's paper over Garrison's *Liberator* also reveals the political activist temperament of California's African-American communities. While Garrison favored non-violence in abolitionism during the 1850s, Douglass suggested political action for abolitionists. This found a receptive audience among California's African-Americans. For further discussion, see Lapp, *Blacks in Gold Rush California*, 188-189.

22. *The Pacific Appeal*, 12 April 1862, p. 2.

23. *Proceedings of the First State Convention of the Colored Citizens*, 57-58.

24. *Address of the State Executive Committee to the Colored People of the State of California* (Sacramento: 1859), 12.

25. *The Elevator*, 5 May 1865, p. 1. The *Elevator* first began to publish in April, 1865.

26. J. William Snodgrass, "The Black Press in the San Francisco Bay Area, 1856-1900," *California History* 60 (Winter 1981/1982): 306-317. Between 1856 and 1900 there were seven African-American newspapers published in the San Francisco Bay area.

27. *The Pacific Appeal*, 1 August 1863, pp. 2-3.

28. *Mirror of the Times*, 22 August 1857, p. 2.

29. Jenkins, "White Racism and Black Response in California History," 125.

30. For information concerning the 1856 sessions of the State Executive Committee, see the *Pacific Appeal*, 19 April, 1862, p. 2. The 1857 resolutions are covered in the *Pacific Appeal*, 5 May 1862, p. 2. The homestead issue is discussed in the *Pacific Appeal*, 20 Sept. 1862, p. 2.

31. *Address of the State Executive Committee to the Colored People*, 15.

32. Philip M. Montesano, "San Francisco Black Churches in the Early 1860's: Political Pressure Group," *California Historical Quarterly* 52 (Summer 1973): 147.

33. *Pacific Appeal*, 4 April 1862, p. 1.

34. *Pacific Appeal*, 5 May 1862, p. 2.

35. *Pacific Appeal*, 13 Sept. 1862, p. 2; *Pacific Appeal*, 7 Feb. 1863, p. 2.

36. *Pacific Appeal*, 12 April 1863, p. 2. Governor Leland Stanford strongly supported the Union cause during his term in office (1862-63).

37. *Pacific Appeal*, 27 April 1862, p. 2.

38. Lawrence P. Crouchett, Lonnie G. Bunch, III and Martha Kendall Winnacker, *Visions Toward Tomorrow: The History of the East Bay Afro-American Community 1852-1977* (Oakland: Northern Center for Afro-American History and Life, 1989), 4.

39. *Pacific Appeal*, 26 April 1863, p. 2; *Elevator*, 6 September 1867, p. 2.

40. *Elevator*, 14 August 1868, p. 2.

41. *San Francisco Elevator*, 24 January 1867, p. 2.

42. *San Francisco Elevator*, 31 July 1868, p. 2.

43. *Ibid.*, 2.

44. *Elevator*, 30 August 1867, p. 2.

45. Limerick, *The Legacy of Conquest*, 262.

46. Oakland's Board of Education became the first to integrate its public school system within the state. Three years later, San Francisco followed Oakland's example. Goode, *California's Black Pioneers*, 85; Crouchett, Bunch, and Martha Kendall Winnacker, *Visions Toward Tomorrow*, 4-5.

47. Fisher, "The Political Development of the Black Community," 260.

48. Crouchett, Bunch, and Winnacker, *Visions Toward Tomorrow*, 5.

49. Lapp, *Blacks in Gold Rush California*, 182-183.

50. *Pacific Appeal*, 16 Dec. 1871, p.2; *Pacific Appeal*, 10 Feb. 1872, p. 2.

51. Fisher, "The Political Development of the Black Community, 39.

52. Alexander Saxton, *The Indispensable Enemy: Labor and the Anti-Chinese Movement in California* (Berkeley and Los Angeles: University of California Press, 1971), 80-82.

53. *San Francisco Examiner*, 1-13 July 1867, 1.

54. *Alta California*, 4 May 1867, 1.

55. Edward Everett France, *Some Aspects of the Migration of the Negro to the San Francisco Bay Area Since 1940* (Berkeley: University of California, 1962; repr. R and E. Research Associates, 1974), 17.

56. Crouchett, Bunch, and Winnacker, *Visions Toward Tomorrow*, 2.

57. Brainerd Dyer, "One Hundred Years of Negro Suffrage," *Pacific Historical Review* 37 (1968): 8.

58. *Ibid.*, 9.

59. France, *Some Aspects of the Migration of the Negro*, 17. This view ignores the strong opposition in California to the Chinese, who by 1870 outnumbered African-Americans by a population of 49,000 to 4,200. California State Senator, William M. Gwin, Jr., from Calaveras County (son of a former U.S. Senator and Chivalry Democrat, William M. Gwin) stated this antagonism to the Chinese quite succinctly when he said on January 13, 1870 that the whites in California would be degraded by the Fifteenth Amendment to the level of blacks and Chinese. "The Chinese population among us is composed almost entirely of males. Of sixty-five thousand Chinese in this State at least fifty thousand are men of voting age." Fisher, "The Political Development of the Black Community," 45.

60. Crouchett, Bunch, and Winnacker, *Visions Toward Tomorrow*, 10.

61. Fisher, "The Political Development of the Black Community, 40.

62. Theodore H. Hittell, *History of California* 4 (San Francisco: N.J. Stone & Co., 1897), 59.

63. Warren A. Beck and David A. Williams, *California: A History of the Golden State* (Garden City, New York: Doubleday & Company, Inc., 1972), 162.

64. *San Francisco Pacific Appeal*, 14 March 1863, p. 2; *San Francisco Pacific Appeal*, 9 May 1863, p. 2; *San Francisco Pacific Appeal*, 30 May 1863, p. 2.

65. Phil Montesano, *The Black Churches in Urban San Francisco, 1860-1865: Their Educational, Civic, and Civil Rights Activities*, TMs [1968], The Bancroft Library, University of California, Berkeley, 1.

66. Dyer, "One Hundred Years of Negro Suffrage," 8.

67. *San Francisco Elevator*, 21 May 1869, p. 2.

68. Starr, *Americans and the California Dream*, 374-375.

69. The A.M.E. Church was established by Philadelphia Methodists after the American Revolution. The Philadelphia A.M.E. added "Bethel" to their denomination. When black Methodists in New York separated from the white Methodist church in the 1820s they adopted the name "Zion" for their church. Both groups would be represented in the Bay Area.

70. Crouchett, Bunch, and Winnacker, *Visions Toward Tomorrow*, 15.

71. *Ibid.*, 15.

72. *San Francisco Elevator*, 3 July 1886, p. 3.

73. *Proceedings of the First State Convention of the Colored Citizens*, 11.

CHAPTER II

BUILDING COMMUNITY AND ECONOMIC
INDEPENDENCE, 1900-1919

By 1900 over one thousand African-Americans lived in Oakland. This population tripled by 1910, and by 1920 there were over six thousand blacks in Oakland. Migrants to the East Bay during the mid-nineteenth century came from the cotton belt of Texas and Oklahoma looking for work first in the cotton centers of Southern California and then drifting to the north. Southern blacks, tired of "bulldozing" by southern legislatures, continued their exodus to California in ever increasing numbers as jobs made available by the Central and Southern Pacific Railroads and the Pullman Company opened up.[1] As the East Bay began to challenge San Francisco for port dominance at the turn of the century, opportunities for employment among the African-American community increased. Until 1900 most areas for black employment focused on day laborers, waiters, barbers, railroad hands, and some in-service trades. As more people came to settle in the East Bay, community leaders began to urge home ownership and business endeavors which imitated the security and prosperity African-Americans believed existed in white communities. Because *de jure* and *de facto* discrimination against African-Americans still existed in California despite the legal victories of the nineteenth century, black families were required to live in segregated black neighborhoods, refused service in public places, and denied employment opportunities. The African-American communities of the East Bay paralleled but did not integrate with white society.

Oakland black residents noticed a number of newcomers among them after 1898 who came with trade skills and, in some cases, professions. These men were veterans of the Spanish-American War who decided to remain on the West Coast after their military service. Not only did black troopers serve at Las Guasimas, El

Caney, and San Juan Hill in June and July, 1898, but they also served in the Philippines. African-American soldiers from the 24th and 25th Infantries were stationed in the Philippines during the Philippine-American War, 1899-1902. The 25th Infantry steamed out of San Francisco harbor aboard the U.S. Transport *Pennsylvania* on the evening of July 1, 1899, en route to Manila. During their stay in the Philippines African-American communities in the United States exhibited pride that black troops abroad could prove "to the Filipinos that brutality is not always covered by a black skin."[2]

The *Pacific Appeal* carried many articles devoted to covering the activities of the regiments stationed in the Philippines. A permanent station was established at Iba in 1899. On January 5, 1900, two companies of the battalion were attacked at Iba by a brigade of insurgents under General San Miguel. This attack was repulsed without any losses to the American troops while the enemy suffered fourteen dead on the field.[3] Reports on General Lawton's famous chase of the Filipino rebel leader, Aguinaldo, to the Cagayan mountains made their way back to the *Pacific Appeal*, the African-American community of San Francisco, and the East Bay.

When the 24th and 25th Infantries returned to the West Coast some of the men resumed their civilian lives in the Bay Area. In 1902 Dr. William W. Purnell became the second black physician to practice medicine in the East Bay after his return from serving as an army doctor in the Philippines. However, even as other veterans of the Spanish-American War chose to settle in California's East Bay at the turn of the century, the African-American population of the region remained only a small percentage of the total area's population. Political and social contacts between the African-Americans and whites were few as a result of the small minority status. Edward France noted in his study of African-American migration to the East Bay that:

> Most of the better restaurants and hotels served Negroes without discrimination, especially if they came as individuals or in small groups. Even all of these places did not welcome large groups of Negroes requesting dining and dancing facilities. Some accepted Negroes without any indication of reluctance, some provided the services required with obvious dissatifaction, and a few refused service altogether. Places of recreation, if privately owned, frequently refused service to Negroes.[4]

Building Community and Economic Independence

African-Americans in the East Bay were well on their way to building parallel communities to the white populace with which they were not welcome to integrate.

Few avenues of employment were open for African-Americans at the turn of the century. In 1899 the Associated Railroad Employees of California was organized in order to better serve the numerous men already working on the railroads. In 1900 a second southern transcontinental rail line was connected to Oakland by the Santa Fe Railroad which extended on to Richmond. The Redcaps of Oakland and the Dining Car Cooks and Waiters of the Owl line thereby provided one means of employment for blacks in the East Bay. During the period from 1870 through the first decades of the twentieth century railroad employees comprised one-fourth to one-third of the African-American work force with the Oakland local being exceptional in its militancy.[5]

In 1901 the Marine Cooks and Stewards Union organized to open a new avenue of employment for African-Americans. In most cases this was the only way that a black man could go to sea. Even if they had licenses to prove it, those men who had worked in other parts of the world as ships' officers or engineers "could only ship on the West Coast as cooks, stewards, or messmen."[6] One exception was Captain William T. Shorey who commanded whaling vessels from 1887 to 1909. Born in Barbados in 1859 to a Scottish sugar planter and a West Indian creole, Rosa Frazier, Shorey was seventeen when he made his first voyage on a whaling ship from Provincetown, Massachusetts. He was able to rise easily through the ranks at this time because only about one-third of whaling crews by 1876 were American-born.[7] Shorey became a master sailor who by 1886 commanded whaling ships as captain. His crews were multi-racial allowing many black sailors an opportunity to go to sea. Marrying Julia Ann Shelton, daughter of one of San Francisco's most prominent African-American families, he moved to Oakland during the late 1880s. After his retirement from sea in 1909, Shorey became active in the affairs of the Home for Aged and Infirm Colored People. This was the first home for elderly care of African-Americans established in California. Located in Beulah, a suburb of Oakland, it opened its doors in 1892.

Oakland became a transportation center not only because it served as the terminus for transcontinental railroads, but also because its great pier extended approximately two and a quarter miles out into the bay (towards Goat Island) allowing much of the state's wheat crop to be loaded into deep water vessels from Oakland's pier.[8] In 1910 Oakland won its first federal shipbuilding contract. Connected to San Francisco by the Santa Fe Ferryboats, Oakland was touted as "a city of culture, of homes and of great commercial promise."[9] After the earthquake of 1906 San Franciscans looked for new homes in the East Bay. Many African-Americans found housing much harder to locate. In 1907 the *Oakland Sunshine* noted:

> Land bought twenty or thirty years ago for a song has been sold during the past year for a fortune, but there is the same opportunity to buy land now which in a similar period of time can be sold to equal advantage.
> To live in either of the cities [Oakland or San Francisco], it is almost necessary for you to own your own home; rents are high and real estate agents do not care to rent to Negroes.[10]

Employment disruption caused by the earthquake forced many African-American businessmen into bankruptcy. The unemployment rate quickly affected the black labor force as well so that by 1920 few businesses in San Francisco were owned by blacks. Most black laborers were employed in the lowest paid jobs.[11]

Oakland's African-American community experienced housing shortages just as its population began to increase with shipping activities and jobs made available to it by the onset of World War I. Men found themselves rooms by the day in West Oakland's hotels and rooming houses. The *Pacific Coast Appeal* carried advertisements for addresses of rooms for rent in Oakland.

Housing shortages were met by the creation of the Pacific Coast Real Estate and Employment Company of Oakland. This African-American real estate agency served such a large number of clients after the dislocation caused by the 1906 earthquake that other agencies would soon appear to take up the cause of helping blacks buy their own homes.

The black press of the day did not fail to note the increased activity of African-Americans in the East Bay:

> West Oakland is beginning to resemble a bee hive of industry among the colored population. Barber shops, hotels, coal yards,

Building Community and Economic Independence 35

grocery stores, tailor shops, restaurants, club rooms, etc. are among the numerous enterprises of that portion of the Athens city.[12]

In the spring of 1900 several African-American businessmen met to organize "a business organization without politics of any kind . . . ." Men such as Captain William T. Shorey and William Tippton who owned a restaurant and tamale cafe were Oakland organizers of the group which became known as the African-American Co-Operative Association. This group promoted itself as proving "to the Negro race that with little effort and a little energy they can accomplish something in the business field as well as in any other."[13] This association did much to extend the promise of equality between white and black races in the Bay Area. However, it also promoted the idea of self-help within the black community. This ideology paralleled the accommodationist philosophy of Booker T. Washington which became so prominent in the American South during the early twentieth century. By 1919 the Oakland and East Bay Cities Negro Business League organized itself along the lines of Washington's national Negro Business League. The primacy of the African-American Co-Operative Association remained evident throughout the early twentieth century. The association was not only established first, but it also retained a larger number of prominent East Bay leaders devoted to equality than the Negro Business League. The promise of liberation and equality which drove nineteenth century African-Americans to settle in California now appeared to live on in their East Bay descendents.

Social clubs debated the question of integration as early as the turn of the century. "Ladies Debate Race Question" and "Should the Color Line Exist in Women's Clubs?" were regularly debated by the Philomath Club in San Francisco. The *Pacific Appeal* regularly covered the debates and reported on their front page when:

> the affirmative contended that colored women should not be permitted to join the federation, upon the ground that they were not of sufficiently high standard to affiliate with the white sex.[14]

Mutual aid organizations resulted from the expanding sense of community which was catalyzed by the press and churches. In 1899

Fanny Jackson Coppin came to visit Oakland. A native of Washington, D.C., and the first African-American graduate of Oberlin College in 1865, Coppin became the principal of the first Industrial School in Philadelphia. This school predated Tuskegee. Oakland club women were so impressed with Fanny Jackson Coppin that they changed the name of their "Women's Club" to the "Fanny Jackson Coppin Club." It served as the prototype for African-American women's groups in California. Among its various objectives was the entertainment of visitors that came to the West Coast, particularly women.[15] The club believed that "Not failure, but low aim is crime." A number of benefits and social events were hosted by the black women's clubs which followed the lead of the national Federation of Women's Clubs. In 1913 a Northern Federation of Colored Women's Clubs organized and incorporated the Fanny Jackson Coppin Club and other groups. After four years of effort, club women opened the Northern Federation Home and Day Nursery in 1918 which provided an orphanage for black children from age five to fourteen. It is operated today by the City of Oakland as a child care center known as the Fannie Wall Children's Home. More important than the benefits themselves, however, was the faith which African-Americans shared that their social and cultural aspirations gave them opportunities to expand their outlook and create the self-esteem which their often low-status jobs denied them.

Oakland built its renown as a more favorable residence for African-Americans than San Francisco upon its greater employment opportunities and wide network of social affiliations. The *Pacific Coast Appeal* said "It is a city of churches as well as of homes. Sixty-four churches embracing nearly every religious denomination open their doors to the religiously inclined."[16] The black press carried church social announcements and introduced newcomers to the community and church congregation frequently. The church congregations offered leadership opportunities which African-Americans did not receive elsewhere in society. At Oakland's Cooper A.M.E. Zion Church special recognition went to active members and officers of the congregations clubs. Various members belonged to clubs named for leading bishops within the A.M.E. church as well as other groups such as the Independent Sunday School Club and the Railroad Porters Club. The pastor called upon club members to make annual reports as to the financial status of their groups and explain their activities for the benefit of the congregation. These annual church rallies were important events as they measured individual club success. The 1902 rally signalled Mrs. Tobe Williams as a leading member of the congregation as well as Oakland's African-American community because of her outstanding ability to raise funds. She reported that the Bishop G.W. Clinton Club raised $303.05 for the church which the *Pacific Coast Appeal* noted was "unparalleled, so far as church rallies with clubs, are concerned in the Athens of the West."[17] The rallies offered the community a chance to hear eloquent addresses by the various pastors of both East Bay and San Francisco churches. At the 1902 rally the Reverend Tilghman Brown, known as the "Lion of the West," for his oratory and Dr. O.E. Jones, pastor of Oakland's 15th Street A.M.E. Church gave keynote speeches.

The influence of these preachers cannot be underestimated as they were able to combine religious and political themes at will. Well-educated men such as Brown and Jones could explain the ramifications of doctrines affecting the African-American community as well as articulate community issues. Congregations in Oakland and San Francisco fought to recruit the Reverend O.E. Jones to their churches. Educated at Wilberforce University for a teaching career, he taught public school in Kentucky; then he attended Payne Theological Seminary at Wilberforce where he later taught theology. Coming to Oakland's First A.M.E. Church on 15th Street, he soon proved himself to be an eloquent preacher. Finally, San Francisco's Bethel A.M.E. Church recruited the pastor to its congregation. Jones preached not only at church functions but also to various lodges and community groups. In 1904 he addressed the Order of Odd Fellows where he exhorted its members to live blameless and generous lives so that they might earn the high esteem which he described for them from the *Book of Ruth*. The news report of his presentation said that "He referred to the household and of the powerful influence woman has over man. . . . There were many handkerchiefs used to wipe away the tears." The East Bay welcomed charismatic preachers of both sexes. In 1915 the First A.M.E. Church conducted revival services after heartily advertising the appearance of the Reverend Lena Mason of Philadelphia as "the Greatest Woman Evangelist."[18]

However, those ministers who fell short of eloquence at the pulpit fared poorly in the Bay Area. The Reverend J.A. Dennis of

Oakland's Beth Eden Baptist Church had the *Pacific Coast Appeal* befriend him when his parishoners wanted someone more eloquent in preaching. The newspaper reminded the congregation that:

> Neither Christ nor the twelve apostles pleased all that heard them. There are other things to be taken into consideration far beyond the mere mouthings of many would-be preachers, the Christian qualifications and the principles of a man and his financial ability, which is far more important at times than eloquence. In the things which are of the most importance he is not deficient.

The Reverend Dennis was retained by Beth Eden for another year.

By the end of the first decade of the twentieth century, African-Americans in the East Bay assessed their social and political situation to be similar to other black communities throughout the nation. Although avoiding the political disfranchisement which occurred in many states, California's African-Americans remembered their precarious fight to attain the vote and right to testimony and therefore agonized over the race riots breaking out in Atlanta, Georgia, in 1906 and Springfield, Illinois, in 1908.

The following year W.E.B. DuBois founded the National Association for the Advancement of Colored People; within four years of its founding Oakland organized its own chapter of the NAACP. Badly bruised by the national image of African-Americans, NAACP members sought to salvage race pride in the face of stereotypes engineered by best-selling books such as Charles Carroll's *The Negro, A Beast* (1900) and Robert Shufeldt's *The Negro, A Menace to American Civilization* (1906). Not only were former abolitionist journals such as *Atlantic Monthly* now publishing articles touting "the universal supremacy of the Anglo-Saxon" but even the Ku Klux Klan began receiving favorable press when Thomas Dixon published *The Clansman: A Historical Romance of the Ku Klux Klan* in 1905. The Oakland chapter of the NAACP under the leadership of Walter A. Butler led protests against the presentation of the film, *The Birth of a Nation* at Oakland's McDonough Theater in 1917. Letters objecting to the film were sent to the *Oakland Tribune* and a court injunction was obtained by the NAACP. Although its efforts failed to prevent the film from being shown in 1917, the campaign continued and finally succeeded in

1921 when the State of California banned *Birth of a Nation* from circulation. Butler became the chapter's first president and actively undertook a campaign to prevent the Oakland City Council from passing a restrictive housing ordinance preventing African-Americans from buying homes in white neighborhoods.

Numerous proposals by white real estate businessmen for restrictive covenants were made during this period. Finally when an unnaturalized German immigrant proposed an ordinance to the Oakland City Council which would prevent African-Americans from buying real estate in white neighborhoods, the Oakland NAACP brought lawsuits against the city council in order to prevent action upon such ordinances. Butler not only promoted civil rights activism by the Oakland NAACP but he also encouraged civic affairs. He purchased a large block of stock used to finance the Panama Pacific International Exposition in 1915.[19] Oakland's NAACP activities also included legal action to provide African-Americans service in public places such as restaurants and movie theaters. By 1917 the chapter counted over 1000 members.

Some southern states discriminated against African-Americans through use of the Grandfather Clause. Also known as the "old soldier" clause, this stipulated that men who had served in the U.S. army or navy or the Confederate army or navy and their descendants did not have to meet all state qualifications to vote. This meant that many whites often qualified to vote in southern states when they did not meet the state requirements for voting. Many states followed the example of Mississippi's constitution which required all voters to present "satisfactory evidence" that all their taxes were paid and to understand and give a "reasonable interpretation" of the state constitution.

Most African-Americans did not have ancestors who had served in the Union or Confederate armed services; therefore, they often were excluded from the franchise. Although a U.S. Supreme Court decision, Guinn v. the United States, struck down in 1915 the use of the Grandfather Clause most African-Americans did not experience relief from the economic and social ramifications of prejudice. The Court's majority opinion in 1915 stated that the Fifteenth Amendment overruled Oklahoma and Maryland laws barring Negroes from the polls if their ancestors couldn't vote prior to January 1, 1866. However, it was noted by the *Oakland Sunshine* that "states may prescribe literacy and property qualification tests for voters" although the Court held that these tests could not be used as subterfuge to prevent African-Americans from voting.

In Oakland considerable concern mounted in the same year over the apparent inability of blacks to attain civil service jobs:

> It is a much rumored saying that all manner of schemes have been tried by the Commissioners of Oakland to ascertain the nationality of the applicants for positions, and now the order, it is said, has gone forth for every applicant to state his or her nationality.[20]

Not only did African-Americans not obtain civil service jobs as readily as whites, but they also were the first to be dismissed from such jobs in times of retrenchment. The case of Louie Jackson, a Health Department worker who was dismissed under the cut-backs initiated by Mayor Davie, discouraged many blacks in Oakland from trying to fill civil service positions:

> It does appear that these great retrenchment policies for economy hit our members first. We have been informed that there is not a great deal of encouragement in the policy of civil service for the Negro.[21]

Many editorials took up the economic considerations of Booker T. Washington and urged Negroes to go into business and trades rather than relying on "Uncle Sam, the Pullman Company and the railroads." Self-sufficiency within the African-American community became the watchword of the black press. Young men were urged to "roll up your cotton sleeves and learn some trade. We need plumbers, tinners, shoemakers, electricians, etc. and not so many shirt and collar jobs." These "boiled shirt" jobs were discouraged as not advancing "the race."[22]

Despite the dismay which African-Americans experienced with their employment prospects, Bay Area residents viewed the opening of the Panama Pacific International Exposition in February 1915 with renewed hope for the future of their region. The fair celebrated the opening of the Panama Canal and the restoration of San Francisco after its calamitous earthquake and fire of 1906. Architecturally designed to evoke a sense of the grandeur of past Mediterranean civilizations—Greece, Rome, and Byzantiumvm-the

Building Community and Economic Independence 41

Exposition provided Bay Area residents an opportunity to advertise their unique commercial center. Ernest Coxhead, a local architect, expressed this goal when he said:

> What we want to do is to interest the world in our resources, we want them to stay here, invest their money here, and help us to develop the untouched, unparalleled resources that lie at our hands....[23]

Boosterism for the Exposition flourished even in the African-American community. A committee formed by East Bay residents offered tourism services to black visitors to the fair by providing housing, transportation and sight-seeing advice. Not only did the committee facilitate tourism, but it also spared black visitors the humiliation of being refused service at those establishments not open to them.[24] Special pride derived from the honors awarded Virginia Stephens, an Oakland school girl, who submitted to a newspaper contest the winning name for the Exposition-"Jewel City." The name suggested the 432-foot Tower of Jewels which served as the entrance to the Exposition as well as its focal point. Huge "novagems", faceted glass jewels backed by mirrors, hung from wires on the tower while concealed lights flashed color and a "living film of light" upon it. This special effect became known as "The Burning of the Tower" reminiscent of San Francisco's 1906 fire.[25] Despite the glittering symbol of the phoenix city there were reflections of a more somber cast which African-Americans recognized. Although the contest sponsors were pleased with Virginia Stephens' name for the Exposition, when they learned that she was a black teenager only fourteen years old they drastically cut back the honors which they had promised to the contest's winner. Given this slight, it is interesting that Annie Virginia Stephens would go on to become the first black woman to complete a law degree at the University of California in Berkeley. In an article appearing in *Architect and Engineer* racial prejudice disguised as Social Darwinism surfaced as the author argued for gothic architecture instead of Mission style at the fair by claiming that:

> the genius of our civilization is emphatically Anglo-Saxon....
> How grandly it would grace this farthest western frontier of the

civilization of the Anglo-Saxon, where it faces its anti-type, the oriental![26]

Comments such as these were not lost on the African-American community. The *Oakland Sunshine* remarked that:

> The Negro had no one day of his own and no building, etc., and derived but very little benefit outside of a few minor jobs as maids and helpers. The management did not solicit very largely of Negro products. The Hampton Quartet sang a few weeks, but our local promoters were not given any financial aid to put on a single production.[27]

Nevertheless, when San Francisco enlisted the services of the federal government to spare the Palace of Fine Arts after the Exposition ended, even the *Oakland Sunshine* concurred. The criticisms were somewhat harsh since African-Americans participated in the athletic events as well as the exhibits. Henry O. Tanner's painting, "Christ in the House of Lazarus," hung in the Palace of Fine Arts along with Tanner's portrait, painted by a white artist.[28] The Filipino band with its black conductor, Walter Loving, performed at the Presidio and participated in parades with the all black 24th Infantry.

The optimism generated by the Panama Pacific International Exposition for commercial prominence soon was overshadowed by the very real need to provide goods and services for a war-ravaged Europe. The East Bay's federal shipbuilding contracts increased as World War I continued. In February, 1918, Paul Scharrenberg, Secretary-Treasurer for the California State Federation of Labor, urged San Francisco's Labor Council to furnish "the proper government officials lists of competent workmen willing to serve the Government labor."[29] African-Americans found the easiest avenue to employment through government calls for unskilled laborers. It was not at all unusual to see advertisements such as "Mare Island Wants Men—Board of Labor at Mare Island Navy Yard wants men immediately—100 unskilled laborers at $3.60 per diem."[30]

The recruitment of whites into the army left numerous jobs open for African-Americans to fill. In addition, the Oakland Chamber of Commerce pursued war contracts for local businesses which further reduced the labor pool. Migration, once again primarily from southern states experiencing an increasing trend towards segregation and violence, helped to ease the drain on the East Bay's labor pool.

As the agrarian upper class in the South defused the Populist Party's threat of a coalition between black and white lower classes, more and more blacks suffered disfranchisement and lynching. Although the *Chicago Tribune's* annual publications of state and national lynching statistics beginning in 1882 indicated that lynching was a nationwide phenonmenon, almost sixty percent of the total lynchings reported between 1882 and 1903 were African-Americans from the South.[31] The bulk of black migrants moving west to avoid southern violence came to California. Many of the state's shipbuilding firms, iron works, and vehicle manufacturers hired black workers for the first time. Oakland's automobile plants included Chevrolet, DeVaux-Hall, Durant, and Willys-Overland.

Housing shortages for African-Americans in the East Bay increased as the migration continued. Labor councils noted that the housing problem corresponded with the success of the area's shipbuilding program and the furnishing of munitions to the American army. Men working in the Vallejo Navy Yard lived in San Francisco or Oakland because there were no housing facilities near their work. This meant they spent as much as four hours per day travelling to and from their work. The San Francisco Labor Council urged housing construction in order to remedy the problems inherent in long-distance commuting. "This travelling month after month accounts for much lost time as well as tiring the workers to such an extent that their efficiency is impaired."[32]

African-Americans found work for the first time in Richmond's local manufacturing firms where bathroom fixtures and roofing materials were produced yet were unable to secure these products for their own housing construction. Local city officials gave scant attention to black housing shortages although many black workers were retained after the war by the Moore shipyards, Richmond's Standard Oil refinery, and foundries.

World War I established a modern form of political surveillance which also impinged upon the African-American community. The Justice Department and its Bureau of Investigation (becoming the F.B.I. in 1935), Army and Navy Intelligence, the U.S. State and Postal Departments as well as other federal agencies began routine surveillance of "radicals." A young J. Edgar Hoover organized the General Intelligence Division (or "anti-radical division") for the Bureau of Investigation. The widespread black migration from the South to urban industrial centers provided a source of consternation for Bureau officials who believed this black exodus would be manipulated by Republican political machines in the fall elections of 1916. As a result of this fear the Bureau of Investigation began to monitor the political activities of African-Americans, especially those who were socialists and their "radical" publications.[33]

In 1916 the Bureau investigated the *Chicago Defender* because it feared the weekly newspaper encouraged the Great Migration. Other monthly publications—*The Messenger, The Emancipator,* and *The Crusader*—advocated socialism and advocated armed resistance to lynchers and race rioters. These journals were identified by Attorney General A. Mitchell Palmer as "radical" publications requiring close monitoring by the U.S. Government. Palmer labelled A. Philip Randolph, editor of *The Messenger*, as the "most dangerous Negro" in the country and agents vandalized *The Messenger's* office.[34] Even the NAACP's official publication, *The Crisis*, received surveillance while U.S. attorneys were directed to silence it as well as the more "radical" publications. However, Congress refused to enact legislation which would ban these journals.[35] African-American agents were recruited by the Bureau to infiltrate black militant activities and obtain information. During the years of the Red Scare immediately following World War I the Bureau hired its first five black special agents: James Edward Amos, Arthur Lowell Brent, Thomas Lion Jefferson, James Wormley Jones, and Earl E. Titus. These men would also cover the growth of Marcus Garvey's United Negro Improvement Association (UNIA).[36]

Although seven agencies gathered intelligence about black radicalism and had a "gentlemen's agreement" to coordinate their information, only the Office of Naval Intelligence (ONI) worked consistently with the Department of Justice. Both agencies were concerned that black militancy would combine with labor radicalism and communism to create revolutionary tendencies in the United States.[37] Under Rear Admiral A.P. Niblack, the ONI became convinced that Japan sought to cultivate the sympathies of African-Americans in order to encourage saboteurs within the United States. The proclamations of Marcus Garvey fed this belief when he

Building Community and Economic Independence 45

described the Japanese as an oppressed colored people suffering at the hands of white imperialist powers.[38] After World War I and throughout the 1920s, Bureau agents vigorously collected data regarding African-American activities supporting Japan. W.B. Poole recorded in his agent reports to the Bureau in December, 1920, that an African-American minister in Cambridge, Massachusetts, the Reverend McClane, suggested giving aid to the Japanese if they were to go to war against the United States.[39]

One of the most interesting cases investigated by the Bureau resulted from agent activities in California. Agent Fred C. Boden reported receiving a letter from an African-American, Hugh M. McBeth, who was "interested in a fake colony and trying to get young colored men to leave the United States and go to Mexico so as to evade the draft." Boden identified McBeth's associates as Theodore Troy and J.E. Littlejohn. They planned a real estate venture in lower California involving over 13,000 acres of land for $80,000.[40] McBeth, an attorney in Los Angeles, had numerous real estate contacts and frequently visited Mexico. Realizing he was under surveillance, McBeth offered George R. Maynes, Director of Negro Economics in the Department of Labor, information from his Mexican trips which he believed might be of interest to the agency. He reported meeting a German man in Ensenada in June, 1917, who told McBeth:

> I notice that you report to the American Colonel. You don't have to do that. The American people have some of you Negroes fooled, but within the next six months Germany is going to show them that more than half of the American Negroes are on Germany's side and don't care a snap of their finger for the American Government offices who have oppressed them.[41]

Other agents reported the activities in California of an Irish priest, Father Fallon, whose sympathies were pro-German. Father Fallon "carried clippings about Negro lynchings and shows them to the negroes, making remarks that they couldn't possibly have a thing like that in Germany."[42]

As World War I came to an end, agents began to shift their attention from German saboteurs among the African-American population to subversion from Japan. Agent Irving P. Roswell reported that bootblack Tom Brady said Mexico and Japan planned trouble against the United States and "are planning war in California."[43]

Of more immediate concern to the Bureau during World War I was the enforcement of the Conscription Act. Evidence of draft evasion was doggedly pursued until the Bureau's new agents rounded up alleged draft evaders in "slacker raids." Thousands of innocent men were arrested and held for days until relatives could prove their compliance with the conscription laws. Over one thousand case files deal with African-Americans arrested in these "slacker raids."[44] Concern regarding Slackers is exemplified by the actions of District Attorney Galen Nichols of Imperial County. He informed Dave Gershon, the Bureau's agent in San Diego, that a Negro by the name of Hudson Selvage of Imperial did not register on June 5th, 1917. Selvage gave his age as 21 to vote in a wet and dry election held in Imperial, but on June 5th stated that he was not 21 and didn't intend to register. Selvage and his brother left town with no forwarding address.[45]

Ironically, the restrictions placed upon African-Americans in the U.S. armed forces fed whites' belief that blacks would be disloyal to their country. When General John J. Pershing made his punitive expedition into Mexico in 1916 there were black Californians who served with with him in the U.S. Ninth and Tenth Cavalries.[46] Parodoxically, their presence in Mexico with Pershing fed the idea within the Bureau that African-Americans were ready to colonize and give their loyalty to the Mexican government. *The Messenger* frequently advertised the ability of African-Americans to buy property cheaply in Mexico. Under a logo stating "Colored People Own a Home in Mexico," the *Messenger* described "Rich, fertile land, only a few miles from Mexico City, the capital of the Republic, . . . now for sale for $5.00 an acre and up."[47] The U.S. Postal Service under the auspices of the Espionage Act monitored such advertisements and carefully followed the people involved in the real estate ventures. When Americans entered World War I Army policies prevented African-American soldiers from reenlisting. Retiring black soldiers were not replaced by other black recruits. Congressman Thaddeus H. Caraway of Arkansas proposed that any colored person be prevented from enlistment or reenlistment in the military.[48] White fears appeared to be realized in the Houston race riot which occurred in August 1917. After an outbreak of racial tension, provoked by an altercation between black military police and white police officers, over a hundred black army regulars in the Twenty-Fourth Infantry seized Springfield rifles in order to march upon Houston.[49] Fifteen white persons were killed during the evening riot in Houston on August 23, 1917.[50] After the first court-martial of sixty-three soldiers, thirteen men were found guilty of all charges and ordered to be hanged by the neck until dead. W.E.B. DuBois reported their death in the January, 1918, issue of the *Crisis*:

> They have gone to their death. Thirteen young, strong men; soldiers who have fought for a country which never was wholly theirs; men born to suffer ridicule, injustice, and, at last, death itself. They broke the law. Against their punishment, if it was legal, we cannot protest. . . . The shameful treatment which these men, and which we, their brothers, receive all our lives, and which our fathers received, and our children await; and above all we raise our clenched hands against the hundreds of white murderers, rapist and scoundrels.[51]

Two additional court-martials followed. The Washington court-martial of fifteen men accused of participating in the riot and threatening civilian lives ended with five men sentenced to hang. The third and last court-martial prosecuted forty additional soldiers and sentenced eleven to be hanged. This became known as the Tillman court-martial since the trial judge advocate, Major Dudley V. Sutphin, considered Corporal Robert Tillman, one of the four non-commissioned officers on trial in this last court-martial, to be "especially obnoxious."[52] Corporal Tillman had testified for the defense during the first trial and thereby earned the wrath of Major Sutphin.

Proposals to prevent black enlistment engendered controversy amidst both races, since many feared African-Americans would threaten white society under universal military service. Some blacks argued, however, that they should not be expected to fight for a country which prevented them from full social equality.

Not all African-Americans felt this way, however; on April 6, 1917, Oscar Hudson, a black attorney from Los Angeles, petitioned the state legislature to permit him to organize a black regiment. Four volunteer Negro regiments were organized as a result—two in southern California and two in the northern part of the state. The companies were disbanded within a month because the Selective Service Act was passed on May 18, 1917, which allowed blacks to be drafted. When a group of African-American draftees left Oakland for basic training the mayor of Oakland and a city councilman addressed the men and wished them luck in their effort to keep democracy alive abroad. Two days later, as the troops left, the Oakland City Council considered a restrictive housing ordinance for the Santa Fe Tract, a white neighborhood. Both the mayor and councilman who addressed the departing black troops favored the restrictive covenant.[53]

Such inconsistencies plagued the black soldier during World War I. Bulletin No. 35 issued by General C.C. Ballou at Headquarters 92d Division, Camp Funston, Kansas, is one example of the army's acquiescence to racial prejudice. On March 28, 1918, General Ballou's five-point bulletin advised that conflicts which raised "the color question" were to be avoided at all times:

> To avoid such conflicts the Division Commander has repeatedly urged that all colored members of his command, and especially the officers and non-commissioned officers, should refrain from going where their presence will be resented. In spite of this injunction, one of the sergeants of the Medical Department has recently precipitated the precise trouble that should be avoided, and then called on the Division Commander to take sides in a row that should never have occurred had the sergeant placed the general good above his personal pleasure and convenience. This sergeant entered a theater, as he undoubtedly had a legal right to do, and precipitated trouble by making it possible to allege race discrimination in the seat he was given. He is strictly within his legal rights in this matter, and the manager is legally wrong. Nevertheless the sergeant is guilty of the GREATER wrong in doing ANYTHING, NO MATTER HOW LEGALLY CORRECT, that will provoke race animosity.[54]

Recognition of blatant segregation which existed in the U.S. Army convinced German agents that African-Americans could be persuaded to desert their units or to be disloyal to their country. Their hopes never materialized.

As the war wound down, African-Americans began to turn their attention to the liabilities they faced at home. In August 1919 the *Messenger's* cover ran the headline "How to Stop Lynching!" The

Building Community and Economic Independence 49

following month the magazine ran a two-page cartoon showing the advice of the "Old Crowd" Negro opposed to the "New Crowd" Negro. On the first page, Booker T. Washington is caricatured along with other accommodationists watching violence but saying "Be modest and unassuming; When they smite thee on one cheek, turn the other." Under this cartoon ran a caption stating: "Following the advice of the 'Old Crowd' Negro." On the next page, another cartoon was captioned "The 'New Crowd' Negro Making America Safe for Himself." This showed a black soldier in an armed tank firing on whites under a banner stating "Giving the 'Hun' a Dose of His Own Medicine." The black soldier is pictured saying: "Since the government won't stop mob violence, I'll take a hand."[55]

This was a new image of the African-American and the militancy of the "New Crowd" Negro encouraged the growth of radicalism, especially in labor. When the American Federation of Labor held its convention in Atlantic City during June, 1919, it "went on record as endorsing and planning to organize Negroes in the unions throughout the United States."[56] The *Messenger*, under its logo "The only magazine of scientific radicalism in the world published by Negroes," endorsed unionization of black labor. It also supported strike activities when it said:

> The strike is the chief weapon in the hands of labor in the class war, since by the use of it, labor is able to enforce a loss upon capital by arresting production. When production ceases, profits stop also.[57]

The "New Crowd" image for African-Americans also differed from its predecessor in terms of self-esteem. After World War I African-Americans used the broad network of economic, social, and political organizations which they had carefully built in the preceding decades to voice not only their aspirations but also their dissatisfaction. The California Dream for African-Americans entered a new phase of economic militancy.

NOTES

1. Carter G. Woodson, *A Century of Negro Migration* (Washington, D.C., 1918; reprint, New York: AMS Press, 1970), 126. Woodson defined the term "bulldozing" to mean the abridgment of Afro-American political rights. Blacks often found their suffrage in southern states severely restricted. "Bulldozing" often meant violence perpetrated against African-Americans.
2. *San Francisco Pacific Appeal*, 2 August 1902, p. 1.
3. *Ibid.*, p. 4.
4. France, "Some Aspects of the Migration", 18.
5. Tony Molitar, "From Slavery to Amtrak: A History of the Pullman Porters in the East Bay," Paper presented at the Southwest Labor Conference, San Francisco, California, 28 April 1989.
6. "Explorations in Black Maritime History Exhibit," *Maritime Humanities Newsletter* 2 (Spring 1983): 5.
7. E. Berkeley Tompkins, "Black Ahab: William T. Shorey, Whaling Master," *California Historical Quarterly* 51 (Spring 1972): 77. For a statistical breakdown of African-American sailors on the East Coast, see W. Jeffrey Bolster, "'To Feel like a Man': Black Seamen in the Northern States, 1800-1860," *Journal of American History* 76 (March 1990), 1173-1199.
8. Although the *San Francisco Pacific Appeal* in 1904 claimed the Oakland pier was three miles long, a scale map of the Master Mariners Race of 1877 showed the pier as approximately two and a quarter miles. Roger R. Olmsted, *Scow Schooners of San Francisco Bay*, edited by Nancy Olmsted (Cupertino, CA: California History Center, 1988), 36. Silting over a twenty-seven year period could have easily lengthened the pier to maintain its three fathom mark for the loading of deep-water vessels.
9. *San Francisco Pacific Appeal*, 21 December 1901, p. 13; *San Francisco Pacific Appeal*, 19 December 1903, p. 3.
10. *Oakland Sunshine*, 21 December 1907, p. 2.
11. Goode, *California's Black Pioneers*, 109.
12. *San Francisco Pacific Coast Appeal*, 18 January 1902, p. 4.
13. "The Origin of the Afro-American Co-Operative Association of San Francisco," *San Francisco Pacific Coast Appeal*, 3 January 1903, p. 12.
14. *San Francisco Pacific Coast Appeal*, 7 December 1901, p. 1.

15. Joyce Henderson, *Tarea Hall Pittman: NAACP Official and Civil Rights Worker* (Earl Warren Oral History Project, Regional Oral History Office, Bancroft Library, 1974), 53a-54.
16. *San Francisco Pacific Coast Appeal*, 21 December 1901, p. 13.
17. *San Francisco Pacific Coast Appeal*, 30 August 1902, p. 9.
18. *San Francisco Pacific Coast Appeal*, 14 May 1904, p. 4; *Oakland Sunshine*, 26 June 1915, p. 1.
19. Goode, *California's Black Pioneers*, 111-112.
20. *Oakland Sunshine*, 24 July 1915, p. 1; "What of Civil Service and How is the Black Man to be Treated," *Oakland Sunshine*, 13 November 1915, p. 2.
21. *Ibid.*, 2.
22. *Oakland Sunshine*, 16 October 1915, p. 2. When the NAACP established its organization in 1909 it adopted the term "colored people" to identify its members. This term seemed more inclusive but failed to distinguish among members of different races. In 1910 the *Chicago Defender*, the first black-owned national daily newspaper, invented the term "race men" and "the race" to describe Afro-Americans. The paper's owner, Robert Abbott, hated the word "Negro" and detested anything associated with the color black. See Taylor Branch, *Parting the Waters: America in the King Years 1954-63* (New York: Simon and Shuster, 1988), 45.
23. Gray Brechin, "Sailing to Byzantium: The Architecture of the Panama Pacific International Exposition," *California Historical Quarterly* 62 (Summer 1983): 109.
24. Crouchett, Bunch, and Winnacker, *Visions Toward Tomorrow*, 19.
25. Brechin, "Sailing to Byzantium", 112.
26. Racial Darwinism flourished in an environment that Pierre L. van den Berghe has called "the postemancipation 'competitive' stage of race relations. George M. Fredrickson, *The Black Image in the White Mind: The Debate on Afro-American Character and Destiny, 1817-1914* (New York: Harper & Row, Publishers, 1971), 255. For quote, see Gray Brechin, "Sailing to Byzantium: The Architecture of the Panama Pacific International Exposition," *California Historical Quarterly* (Summer 1983): 109.
27. *Oakland Sunshine*, 11 December 1915, p. 2.
28. Goode, *California's Black Pioneers*, 110-111.

29. "Shipbuilding Information," *The Labor Clarion* 17 (8 February 1918): 5.

30. "Mare Island Wants Men," *The Labor Clarion* 17 (19 April 1918): 16.

31. Richard Maxwell Brown, *Strain of Violence: Historical Studies of American Violence and Vigilantism* (New York: Oxford University Press, 1975), 151.

32. *The Labor Clarion* 17 (19 April 1918): 8.

33. Between 1916 and 1930 over one and a half million Afro-Americans left the South to participate in what became known as the "Great Migration."

34. August Meier and Elliott Rudwick, eds., *Federal Surveillance of Afro-Americans, 1917-1925: The First World War, the Red Scare and the Garvey Movement.* Black Studies Research Sources. Microfilms from major archival and manuscript collections (Ann Arbor, Michigan: University Publications of America, 1986), xii.

35. *Ibid.*, xi.

36. *Ibid.*, xiii.

37. *Ibid.*, xvi.

38. *Ibid.*, xvi.

39. Department of Justice, Bureau of Investigation, *Federal Surveillance of Black Americans, 1916-1925.* Casefile BS213522: Negro Relations with Japanese. 1921. [Washington, D.C.: National Archives and Records Administration, RG65, F.B.I. cont.], 0966, microfilm.

40. Department of Justice, Bureau of Investigation, *Federal Surveillance of Black Americans, 1916-1925.* Casefile OG132476: Negro Activities, California. 1918-1920. [Washington, D.C.: National Archives and Records Administration, RG65, F.B.I. cont.], 0135, microfilm.

41. *Ibid.*

42. Department of Justice, Bureau of Investigation, *Federal Surveillance of Black Americans, 1916-1925.* Casefile OG238521: Pro-German Activities. Calif., 1918. [Washington, D.C.: National Archives and Records Administration, RG65, F.B.I. cont.], 0944, microfilm.

43. Department of Justice, Bureau of Investigation, *Federal Surveillance of Black Americans, 1916-1925.* Casefile OG375308: Japanese/Mexican Collaboration, California, 1919, by George T.

Holman, [Washington, D.C.: National Archives and Records Administration, RG65, F.B.I. cont.], microfilm.

44. Meier and Rudwick, *Federal Surveillance of Afro-Americans*, x.

45. Department of Justice, Bureau of Investigation, *Federal Surveillance of Black Americans, 1916-1925*. Casefile OG 30791: Failure to Register, California, 1917. [Washington, D.C.: National Archives and Records Administration, RG65, F.B.I. cont.], 0420, microfilm.

46. Frank E. Vandiver, *Black Jack: The Life and Times of John J. Pershing*, vol. 2 (College Station, Tx. and London: Texas A & M University Press, 1977), 614, 619. The United States 10th Cavalry was the famed "Buffalo Soldier" outfit which had seen action in several Indian skirmishes.

47. Department of Justice, Bureau of Investigation, *Federal Surveillance of Black Americans, 1916-1925*. Records Relating to the Espionage Act, WWI, 1917-1921, U.S. Postal Service [Washington, D.C.: National Archives and Records Administration, RG28], 00699, microfilm.

48. U.S. Congress, House of Representatives, *A Bill to Prevent the Enlistment of Negroes in the Military Service of the United States*, H.R. 17183 64th Congress, 1st session, 1916, pp. 11517-12586.

49. Thirteen died in the Houston riot and nineteen people were wounded. Several companies involved in the riot were from the 24th Infantry which included both regular service men and recent enlistees who came from various parts of the country. Allen D. Grimshaw, ed., *Racial Violence in the United States* (Chicago: Aldine Publishing Company, 1969), 73-87.

50. The Houston race riot was the first in which more whites were killed than blacks and a "conflict between black soldiers and white citizens in which the former made a conscious effort to keep black Houstonians from participating." Robert Haynes, *A Night of Violence: The Houston Riot of 1917* (Baton Rouge: Louisiana State University Press, 1976), 208.

51. *Ibid.*, 274.

52. *Ibid.*, 287.

53. Goode, *California's Black Pioneers*, 116.

54. Emmett J. Scott, *American Negro in the World War* (Chicago: L.W. Walters Co., 1919), 97-101.

55. Department of Justice, Bureau of Investigation, *Federal Surveillance of Black Americans, 1916-1925*. Records Relating to the Espionage Act, WWI, 1917-1921, U.S. Postal Service [Washington, D.C.: National Archives and Records Administration, RG28], 00717-00718, microfilm.

56. "The Negro and the American Federation of Labor," *The Messenger* (August 1919): 10.

57. "Strikes," *The Messenger* (September 1919): 5-6.

CHAPTER III

ECONOMIC MILITANCY CONFRONTS THE DICHOTOMY OF THE CALIFORNIA DREAM, 1920-1939

The decades following World War I presented Californians with a harsh confrontation between their expectations for a better life and the reality of poverty amidst plenty, discrimination, and a legacy of conquest. The California Dream cloned the political and economic aspirations of Spanish and American settlers and wrapped them in the natural luxuriance of California—a state where the environment shaped the outlook of its inhabitants. The natural diversity of the state's resources supported a myriad of economic pursuits which Californians eagerly undertook, always with enthusiasm but sometimes with little wisdom. The era of the 1920s promoted boosterism among the African-American communities of the East Bay, but it also engendered antagonism to forces which restricted the freedom of the African-American to achieve the financial and personal success which the California Dream promised. Black businessmen were highly conscious of impediments to their prosperity and eager to take corrective action. In an article titled "Oakland's Shame," the *California Voice* claimed that:

> the failure of colored business enterprises in our city is really becoming alarming. Folks don't frequent 'race' businesses and clubs and go to facilities owned by 'others' instead of The Community House (owned by members of our group).[1]

Heavily influenced by the growth of the Garvey Movement in the Bay Area, newspapers such as the *California Voice* and the *Pacific Appeal* became staunch advocates of black self-help programs. The United Negro Improvement Association (UNIA) which Marcus Garvey established created an Oakland chapter, Local No. 188, in 1920 for the establishment of self-help programs and black nationalism within the community. J.E. Crummer served as the local's first president. On the same day that the *California Voice* decried the shame of Oakland it also advertised the arrival and pending lectures in Oakland of Captain E.L. Gaines of New York City. Captain Gaines, a Minister of Legion for the UNIA, spoke on the "Objects and Aims of the UNIA" at Oakland's Beth Eden Baptist Church.[2] Already responsive to the self-help philosophy of the UNIA, Oakland residents turned out in large numbers on June 4-5, 1922 when Marcus Garvey spoke there as part of his California tour.

At his first Oakland speech, there were six detectives from the Department of Justice's Bureau of Investigation in the audience. Asked by his Oakland promoters whether he wanted them removed, Garvey declined and went on with his speech.[3] Denouncing white racism and supremacy in the United States, Garvey stressed the need for unity among "colored races."

Visiting lecturers at the UNIA meetings often came from India and East Asia to highlight the need for global solidarity among people of color. The Bureau of Investigation closely monitored the activities of the UNIA and followed the publications of the *Ethiopian* published in Oakland. The *Digest* served as the official organ of the UNIA on the West Coast. Although there was antagonism from some NAACP and Negro Business League leaders who viewed Garveyism as a threat to racial integration, the UNIA in the East Bay persevered despite the misfortunes of its leader. While the *Oakland Sunshine* ran editorials in 1922 urging rejection of the UNIA for its doctrine of racial separatism, many avowed integrationists such as Delilah Beasley, black reporter for the *Oakland Daily Tribune*, and Frances Albrier, a Black Cross Nurse and vice-president of the Women's Auxiliary in 1923, supported the UNIA as well as other organizations for racial improvement. Albrier believed that the UNIA's insistence upon black pride and self-help did not detract from integration efforts.[4]

The Black Cross nurses, under the direction of the Women's Auxiliary, secured financial aid for community members needing medical assistance, taught health and hygiene classes, and circulated among the community to bolster moral support in the UNIA movement. Since the American Red Cross in World War I excluded black nurses, the services of the Black Cross Nursing Corps offered black women an opportunity to use their skills professionally.

Albrier remembered her excitement and racial pride when she joined the UNIA Women's Auxiliary:

> I had a long talk with Mr. Garvey when he came out here with some of his people from his office in New York, about the movement and why he was proposing separate races. Mr. Garvey was an internationalist; he was from Jamaica. He was comparing the Negro people in the United States, and the Negro people in the West Indian Island, and the Negro people in black Africa. He saw how they were *all* exploited. He said that the reason they were not elevated and were not able to get up and be somebody in the world as a race, was because they were all so separated. They all saw through the eyes of different nations and different nationalities. They only continent they knew was their continent, where their roots were, was Africa.[5]

Separated from her husband, William Albert Jackson, and mother of three children by 1926, Frances found that unpaid public service for the Black Cross Nurses Corps could not sustain her family; so she began working as a maid for the Pullman Company. However, her view of Garvey's UNIA movement continued to influence Frances Albrier's political activism throughout her life.

Delilah Beasley's race pride antedated the UNIA by several years. She came to California from Ohio in 1909 with the intent to write a book on Negro activities in the state. Studying California history at the University of California in Berkeley for nearly six years she supported herself through the practice of scientific massage. In 1915 Delilah Beasley wrote articles for the *Oakland Daily Tribune* about exhibits by African-Americans at the Panama Pacific International Exposition. During the war years she wrote *The Negro Trail Blazers of California* which was published in 1919. It remains today as one of the most comprehensive studies of Negroes in nineteenth and early twentieth century California. After the formation of the Oakland chapter of the UNIA, Beasley became interested in journalism once again. In 1923, she began writing a weekly column called "Activities Among the Negroes" for the *Oakland Daily Tribune*. Within this column, she strove to abolish the use of the denigrating words "darkey" and "nigger" in print. The Knowland family which owned and published the *Tribune* gave her their cooperation along with that of the paper's editorial staff.[6] She wrote this column until her death in 1934. With Beasley's public wrote this column until her death in 1934. With Beasley's public relations support and community leadership behind it, the Oakland UNIA local survived even the deportation of Marcus Garvey after 1927. Oakland's UNIA local drew large crowds for its Garvey Day celebrations well into the 1930s. The *California Voice* proclaimed "the spirit of Garveyism . . . in full evidence" when a large audience gathered at the Shrine of Liberty (Liberty Hall at Chester and Eighth Streets in Oakland) to renew vows of "African Nationalism."[7]

Enthusiasm for black pride in civic issues also stemmed from African-American students attending the University of California at Berkeley. By the 1920s black students at Berkeley organized campus social groups such as the Rho Chapter Alpha Kappa Alpha Society and the Acorn Club. Rho Chapter formed in 1921 and became the first organized Kappa Chapter of the Delta Sigma Theta Sorority. According to Lawrence P. Crouchett:

> For black students, sororities and fraternities at Berkeley—whose members included both students and university graduates—were a critical source of support. Not only did they provide a context for social life, but they created a direct link to the community. Adult members were keenly aware of the position they occupied as role models and vocational counselors and continually reinforced the students' sense of purpose and commitment. Black students also used their "Greek" organizations to insert themselves into campus life in ways which they hoped would win recognition for them. In 1930, when the university was building Cowell Memorial Hospital, it asked for donations, designating $300 as the cost of furnishing one room. Although a few years earlier they had not had enough money to have their photographs taken for the *Blue and Gold* yearbook, the Delta Sigma Theta sorority and Omega Psi Phi fraternity each contributed $150. The fund-raising drive, which was materially assisted by the black churches, reflected a persistent belief that blacks could overcome racial discrimination by their attainments and contributions.[8]

Black graduates of Berkeley such as Walter A. Gordon acted as "race" emissaries by living exemplary lives of service not only within their African-American communities but also in the civic affairs of the East Bay. Gordon grew up in San Bernardino and went to U.C.

Berkeley during World War I. At Cal Gordon played football for Coach Andy Smith's "Wonder Teams" and became one of the first players west of the Rockies to receive honorable mention in the All-American roster.[9] The campus employed Gordon after his 1918 graduation as an assistant coach for its football team. When he went on to become the first black officer on the Berkeley Police Force, he was given time off every year to coach and scout for Cal.

When Walter Gordon attended law school in the early 1920s, he became a close friend of Earl Warren who began his career as District Attorney for Alameda County and later as Chief Justice of the U.S. Supreme Court during the *Brown vs. Board of Education, Topeka* case. Gordon's access to Warren helped further civil rights issues in California which the two men discussed over the decades when Warren served as Attorney General and then as Governor of California. Walter Gordon's strength among white political circles stemmed not only from his athletic prominence but also from his discretion which made whites feel at ease with him. What this discretion cost him is suggested by colleagues who remember that when Cal took its football teams on the road, Gordon would arrange for his own accommodations at hotels or the homes of black people rather than push for integrated accommodation with Cal's team. Later he would quietly appear in time for the game.[10] Although a key to Gordon's political popularity, his ability to be unobtrusive made him suspect in the eyes of more vocal leaders within the African-American community.[11]

Other African-American students at Berkeley during the 1920s were also committed to civic improvement and racial equity. Tarea Hall Pittman and William Byron Rumford were part of the small coterie of black students at Cal in the 1920s. Arriving on campus in 1923 Tarea (Ty) Pittman found that private homes provided the only housing available for black students as they were not allowed to live in the dormitories.[12] Some of the black male students received board and room at fraternity houses where they worked as waiters. Tarea Pittman lived in the home of Alice Osborne (mother of a former black student at Cal) until 1925. When an Oakland theater showed the film, *Birth of a Nation*, Pittman remembers protesting at the Alameda Courthouse with members of the Oakland NAACP. During this period, 1923-1925, she recalled the African-American protest about blackface minstrel shows in the Bay Area.[13] Pittman's student activism helped to prepare her for a distinguished career as a social worker in the East Bay as well as continued political activism on behalf of African-American civil rights.

William Byron Rumford's black student activism began with his college career at the University of California's College of Pharmacy. Admitted to the College of Pharmacy, located in San Francisco, in the late 1920s, Rumford parked cars at North Beach's elegant Roof Garden Club (later Finocchio's) in order to earn money for his education.[14] After graduating in 1931, Rumford became the pharmacist-owner of Rumford's Pharmacy in Berkeley and later ran successfully for State Assemblyman. His interest in politics grew when he joined the "Appomatox Club" in Berkeley. Designed to support and promote candidates favorable toward issues of importance for the African-American communities of the Bay Area, the Appomatox Club formed in the early 1920s and would serve Bay Area African-Americans for several decades. Rumford recalls efforts by the club to help elect a black city councilperson for Berkeley in campaigns for Tom Berkley and Frances Albrier.[15]

While black students at Berkeley began to organize for political voice, African-Americans in the greater East Bay experienced a wave of evangelical enthusiasm during the 1920s. The *California Voice* reported the work of the "Black Billy Sunday" and Dr. John Snape, pastor of the First Baptist Church at 20th and Telegraph Streets in Oakland. These preachers of the gospel were Oakland's most popular pastors among African-Americans. The Reverend J. Gordon McPherson of St. John's Baptist Church at 32nd and Linden Streets earned the name "Black Billy Sunday" because he was thought to be a "matchless preacher of old-time gospel." The *Voice* claimed the Reverend McPherson performed "great work breaking down bars of prejudice and cementing the races as never before."[16] The significance of preachers and religion must not be played down when reviewing the civil rights activism of African-Americans. Even California claimed its own firebrand leaders who maintained and encouraged a militancy on race issues which did not cease upon threat of arrest. C.L. Dellums, a young man when he came to California from Texas in 1923, remembers visiting his brother, William, in 1920-21 at the time of the Tulsa riots. The bail posted for William Dellums, known as one of the African-American leaders of the riot in Tulsa, amounted to $10,000. With Dellums in jail was H.T.S. Johnson, a black minister who refused to leave jail when a prominent white Tulsa minister went to bail him out. H.T.S. Johnson, who later moved to California, refused bail as a matter of principle saying that he:

> would not leave as long as some white man had to vouch for him, that he would not leave the tag on him, and that he still considered himself a free American and slavery had been abolished![17]

When Johnson arrived in the East Bay he became minister of Parks Chapel Church, built at 9th and Chester Streets in Oakland in 1920 for the A.M.E. Church. Soon elected to the presidency of the Oakland Branch of the NAACP, Johnson continued to impress upon his congregation a sense of self-esteem which did not tolerate racial inequity.

The decade of the 1920s witnessed a heightened sense of racial consciousness which both ministers and social organizations fostered in California. The *California Voice* reported in 1921 that Mrs. Florence Kelley, member of the Oakland NAACP Board and Secretary of the Consumer's League, attended a Pan-African Conference in London where the keynote address given by W.E.B. DuBois focused upon "World Union."[18] C.L. Dellums joined the Northern California Branch of the NAACP in 1924. He helped to form the Alameda County Branch, NAACP, which later split into the Oakland, Berkeley, and Alameda Branches. For Dellums and many other Bay Area blacks, the NAACP retained primacy as the leading organization supporting racial equality. Although an important leader within the Brotherhood of Sleeping Car Porters, Dellums endorsed the NAACP fervently when he said:

> All of us of the Brotherhood always maintained, 'Don't put us Number One!' The National Association for the Advancement of Colored People is the Number One organization of the race, because all of us are a part of the National Association. The National Association is the greatest and the biggest civil rights organization in the world. The National Association is the one organization whose only dedication is *complete, total equality*.[19]

The Oakland NAACP committed its organization to equality when it protested segregation in the policy of the Oakland Playground Department. When directors of a playground refused the right of a black school girl to participate with her class during a public school Christmas Pageant at an Oakland playground, the NAACP protested that this represented segregation by public officials partially paid by taxes from the African-American community. The resolution of this protest in 1925 came when an investigating committee of five heard from the Superintendent of the Playground Department, Jay B. Nash, that no problem existed. Superintendent Nash admitted that directors of playgrounds had not been informed that colored children could participate in special events with their classes but that this information would henceforth prevail in all public playgrounds in Oakland. Nevertheless, African-American children still found playgrounds off-limits to them unless they came with their classmates in a school-authorized activity.[20]

Many East Bay black women joined another organization which promoted civic pride and followed guidelines similar to those of the NAACP. The National Association of Colored Women (NACW) met with Federated Women's Clubs in Oakland during the summer of 1926. Oakland's recently-built Civic Auditorium hosted the 15th Biennial Session for the NACW while over 1500 black club women from Federated Women's Clubs convened there for a week of presentations and delegate meetings from July 31 to August 5, 1926. The concerns of delegates to this convention included public welfare work, educational progress, and "social uplift in their communities." Urging their delegates to train their minds "to be alert for new methods of advancing the progression of Race Women," the NACW under the national leadership of Mary McLeod Bethune encouraged black women's clubs in the Bay Area to fuller participation in civic activities.[21] Four years later the Fifteenth Street A.M.E. Church hosted a California State Convention of Women's Clubs and highlighted the participation of California's black women's clubs in their communities. The California State Association of Colored Women's Clubs first convened in 1908 when the organization's first president was inaugurated. Clubs from southern California, the Art and Industrial Club, and Oakland's Fanny Jackson Coppin Club participated in this first meeting. Tarea Pittman would continue this tradition of community service in the mid-1930s when she became president of the California State Association of Women's Clubs

(1936-38). Pittman, always anxious to bring black women into political activity, achieved success in converting Tehachapi prison from an all-male institution to a separate women's maximum security prison.[22] African-American club women worked toward lessening the overcrowding in Oakland's county jail at First and Broadway where Tarea Pittman remembers the jail as "absolutely horrible!"[23] Women's organizations viewed this as a means of protecting lesser offenders from the detrimental influence of more hardened criminals. The club women even went to see the sheriff in order to encourage reform. After this attack on overcrowded jail conditions, Oakland's Sheriff's Department did hire five African-American women as deputies for the jail.[24]

Still another community-service organization which flourished during the late 1920s and '30s was the Linden Branch Young Women's Christian Association. The national YWCA and YMCA restricted membership to whites only until the early 1920s when the organizations authorized "colored" branches under the authority of local white YWCAs and YMCAs. The Linden Center YWCA organized in 1920 after a group of black women promoted the idea of creating a center where youth could meet free from the dangers of street life. The Linden Center undertook religious and vocational training as well as adult education and recreational and cultural programs. During the 1930s the Linden Branch offered its services as a job placement agency. When Miss Ruth P. Moore arrived in Oakland from Pittsburgh in 1933 as the new YWCA Secretary reporters quickly questioned her on her opinions as to whether she noted a difference between Eastern and Western girls. Although reluctant to answer, Miss Moore indicated that California's:

> golden sunshine made the Western girl a more athletic type with the great outdoors while the eastern city, being congested, makes the Eastern girl more liable to seek pleasure and jazz to pacify her wants.[25]

Her comments regarding jazz seemed especially fitting as a bellwether of the more serious-minded and pragmatic approach to life which the depression decade of the 1930s evoked as opposed to the more carefree views of the 1920s. Responding to a question on her musical preferences, Miss Moore said, "Oh! jazz. I never let that enter my mind; I am too busy with the serious things of life to give an intelligent answer on the subject."[26]

African-American boosterism still flourished as late as 1938 when the Linden YWCA raised $630 in a a funds drive launched by the Golden State Mutual Insurance Company, a black-owned company with over 1500 policy holders in the Bay Area. Active in many community endeavors, the Linden YWCA sponsored a college football tournament for Bay Area players. Sports, although largely segregated, offered African-Americans an opportunity to experience bonhomie among the many Bay Area communities now established around Oakland and San Francisco. When the baseball season opened in May, 1926, the Oakland Colored Giants played Richmond's "fast" Pullman Club. This chance to learn first-hand through players from other communities what their problems were did not go unnoticed by those interested in civil rights. Forced to play other "colored" teams, the Oakland Colored Giants soon knew the issues which prevailed among other minority races in the Bay Area. When they played the Japanese All-Stars of Alameda, African-Americans learned how other minority communities dealt with restrictions upon their civil rights.[27]

During the decades of the 1920s and early 1930s African-Americans in California's East Bay prepared for the struggles which they would face in order to achieve their vision of the justice and equality which their California Dream held. Their preparations included creating parallel social and political institutions to those white communities built for the promotion of civil rights. The black communities of the East Bay saw themselves as builders of educational and mutual aid centers which would struggle against racial restrictions and prejudice until the structures of the dominant white society admitted them. Their unremitting search for the promises of a color-blind California Dream found some satisfaction by the late 1920s when the "Grandfather clause" and the prohibition against blacks voting in Texas Democratic primaries were found unconstitutional by the Supreme Court.[28]

By the 1930s the focus of African-American communities began to center upon challenging "the Supreme Court's separate-but-equal reading of American constitutional justice."[29]

Before the challenge could be mounted at the federal level, however, African-Americans needed to explore and exhaust the options open to them within their own communities. Many settled

Economic Militancy

in Oakland's East Bay during the 1920s and '30s in order to forward their ambitions. C.L. Dellums remembers coming to California when he was 23 years old and choosing "San Francisco as the most ideal place for a Negro to live in 1923."[30] Deciding that he wanted to study law at UC, Berkeley, Dellums took the day coach to San Francisco where he talked to the porter about his aspirations. The porter said:

> Let me give you some advice, young man. Get off in Oakland. There are not enough Negroes in San Francisco for you to find [them] in order to make some connections over there. Worst of all, you will never find a job. The few Negroes around here in the Bay District are in Oakland, so you can make some contacts.

The porter then suggested that Dellums take a room from a lady in West Oakland for $3.00 a week.[31]

When he arrived in Oakland, Dellums quickly learned the axiom that there were only three types of employment for Negroes there: you could go down to the sea in ships, work on the railroads, or do something illegal. The steamship companies in the Bay Area employed large numbers of African-Americans; the *Western American* reported over 250 race men working for the Luckenbach Steamship Company in 1926.[32] Dellums took his first job hiring onto the coastwide ships of the Pacific Steamship Company which ran from British Columbia to San Diego. His job as a room steward paid $45 a month. Dellums disliked the fact that all the Negro help "had to live like cattle in the Glory Hole," a room aboard ship which had bunk beds stacked three-high surrounding the interior walls of the room.[33] While aboard ship, Dellums would read copies of *The Messenger* which he bought whenever his ship put into port in Seattle. For Dellums *The Messenger* represented the leading liberal magazine in the nation during the early 1920s. He read its editorials religiously and found himself favorably impressed with those written by A. Philip Randolph. Soon tired of the segregation and poor conditions he received on board ship, Dellums tried get employment as a waiter in the dining cars of the Southern Pacific. Finding that hiring of crew during winter was extremely difficult, Dellums noticed that the white official who made hiring decisions on the Southern Pacific belonged to a Masonic lodge. As a member of the Prince Hall Masons, Dellums knew the Mason signal for distress; so he gave the white official the Mason sign of distress and finally was hired as a porter for the Pullman Company in January 1924. Dellums was paid $60 a month.[34]

Within the year Dellums became militant in his dealing with the Pullman Company. Dismayed by the inequitable pay scale and corruption he witnessed, Dellums began to force change in the sign-out procedures. The Pullman Company paid men $60 by the calendar month so it did not matter whether a porter worked 485 hours in a month or only 350 hours, he received the same pay. The company never started a porter's pay on p.m. time which meant if a porter was called in to work in the afternoon, his pay wouldn't begin until midnight.[35] In Oakland the Pullman Company had a sign-out booth where a company clerk assigned trips to the porters. Dellums watched porters insure themselves more trips by returning from assignments and handing the clerk a magazine and saying, "There's a good story on page 100." Inside the magazine, the clerk would find a kickback.[36] Dellums's personal campaign for the Brotherhood began with the sign-out booth which originally was nothing more than a small shed to keep the clerk dry in wet weather. Dellums began going inside the booth telling the clerk that as long as he was inside, he'd come in too. Finally the clerk turned to all the men outside and invited them to come inside. Within a few months the Pullman Company found a little house at the end of Wood Street and began renting it for a sign-out office and put in benches for the waiting men.[37] Finding Dellums too militant after he joined the fledgling Brotherhood of Sleeping Car Porters (BSCP) in 1925, the Pullman Company fired him in 1928.[38] He soon became a trouble-shooter for the Brotherhood in Oakland and coined a phrase to keep the Oakland porters united. He would use it often, asking men: "What do you have to lose? You've only got four things anyway: a hard job, low pay, long hours, and a mean bossman! That's all you've got. What if you do lose it?"[39] Collecting dues for the BSCP in an old Model T Ford at porter's homes in the night, Dellums learned that wives resented the threat which they believed the Brotherhood represented to their husbands' job security. He began to talk to porters at the station when they returned from their trips so as to collect dues from the tips which they made on their run. It was not easy to recruit members as many black leaders viewed the Brotherhood with skepticism since they felt the porters were biting the hand that fed them.[40] The Pullman Company was one of the few employers in the 1920s that hired blacks. By 1929 one-third of all black wage-earners in Oakland were railroad employees. Dellums remained proud that "In the darkest of days, Oakland maintained the highest dues-paying membership percentage-wise."[41]

C.L. Dellums met A. Philip Randolph for the first time in January 1926 when Randolph spoke at Parks Chapel Church in West Oakland. Dellums went to the meeting with a preconceived belief that real revolutionaries were always thin men; so he was not surprised to see in Randolph so thin a man "that once in a while he put his hand on his hip and it would gradually slide down. He was so thin, he didn't have a hip."[42] After meeting Randolph, Dellums took on the job of Secretary-Treasurer for the Oakland BSCP local in return for a $25 payment on his rent. In July Randolph raised his pay to $25 a month.[43] The slogan of the Brotherhood became, "A winner never quits and a quitter never wins." Dellums believed in the slogan and the BSCP. During the late 1920s the Brotherhood represented the only national Negro labor organization in America. Soon Dellums found himself the first Negro to be elected a member of the Executive and Arbitration Committee for the Central Labor Council of Alameda County. Adamantly opposed to racial inequity, Dellums utilized every opportunity to open doors previously closed to Negro patronage. One such opportunity came in the late 1920s after a shooting at a white dance in Sweet's Ballroom, the leading dance hall in Oakland. Dellums asked to book the whites-only ballroom for the BSCP after the shooting incident occurred. He not only received permission to use the ballroom but also rented it for a good price when he refused to pay "color tax."[44]

Dellums brought this attitude of adamant militancy into his work for the Brotherhood of Sleeping Car Porters as well. In April 1928 the BSCP took a strike vote which it hoped would result in a declaration of an emergency situation by the National Board of Mediation.[45] The Railway Labor Act stipulated that should such an emergency be declared the President of the United States should appoint an emergency board to settle the dispute and prevent a strike. However, the Board of Mediation argued that a national emergency had not been created by the BSCP's strike vote and therefore the President could not intervene. In the meantime

Dellums asked Bill Spooner, the head of Alameda's Labor Council, for advice about strikes. Spooner sent him to people who knew how to organize and conduct strikes. They told him one day before the strike was to occur that "trains may leave West Oakland but they'd never reach the boats." Since there were no bridges across the Carquinez Straits in 1928, the trains had to be broken up and put on ferry boats to cross the Carquinez Straits where they would then proceed northward or eastward. Dellums believed these people were Communists and would see that the ferry boats did not successfully cross the Straits.[46] Since Dellums was not a Communist, he was relieved when A. Philip Randolph and William Green of the American Federation of Labor (AFL) met to discuss the strike vote and negotiate possible ways to avoid the strike. Green sent a long telegram to the BSCP asking the Brotherhood to call off the strike while the AFL sat down with them to work out a way to help the BSCP. As a result of these negotiations the BSCP obtained thirteen charters from the AFL to affiliate with it (not all local unions affiliated, however). When the BSCP went into the AFL roughly half the AFL unions had color clauses in their constitutions. Nevertheless, the BSCP affiliated with the AFL because it represented the mainstream of the labor movement, and the BSCP believed it belonged in the mainstream as well.[47] Beginning in 1929 A. Philip Randolph gave annual speeches at AFL conventions urging the unions to remove color clauses. William Green supported Randolph at the conventions as he was personally opposed to discrimination in the unions.[48]

When the International Brotherhood of Sleeping Car Porters formed in September 1929 after its first convention in south Chicago, C.L. Dellums was elected Vice-President.[49] None of the delegates to the convention could be Pullman porters because the Pullman Company did not recognize the BSCP at that time. It was not until 1937, twelve years after the Brotherhood's founding, that the Pullman Company signed its first agreement with the BSCP. On August 25, 1937, the BSCP received from its agreement with the Pullman Company the following provisions:

1. Establishment of the standard 8-hour day and 240 hours a month

2. Overtime if a porter worked over the standards

Economic Militancy 69

    3.   Guaranteed layover rest period for porters. If worked on a rest period, porters had to be paid for it.

    4.   A nominal pay increase of $12 a month[50]

The Pullman porters achieved middle-class standing in their communities, because they were regarded as possessing careers, not just day-jobs.

The Pullman Company offered jobs for black women as well as men. Frances Albrier remembered working for the Pullman Company in the late 1920s:

> The only thing I had to learn was manicuring. One of the other maids got a beauty operator to teach me manicuring. That's what the maids did. They took care of the showers for the women who wanted showers and did the manicuring for both men and women.[51]

A maid's first year of employment with the Pullman Company was called "running wild" because the company would schedule maids wherever they were needed. Frances recalled starting out on the Overland train and then taking over for a sick maid on the Twentieth Century once she arrived in Chicago. After one year of service, maids could bid on a regular route if there were vacancies. Leaving her three children with a friend in Berkeley, Frances worked the Sunset Limited route from San Francisco to New Orleans from 1927 to 1931 when the company began to see maids as "an extravagance" the Depression era could ill afford.

Ten days before the Stock Market crashed in 1929, an editorial in the *Oakland Independent* advocated concentration of buying power by African-Americans in the Bay Area in order to encourage the enlargement of economic employment for Negro men and women. Taking its cue from the *Chicago Whip*, the *Oakland Independent* surveyed places of business where African-Americans spent money only to find that many did not employ blacks.[52] According to the 15th United States Census of 1930 there were 7,503 African-Americans living in Oakland while 2,177 lived in Berkeley. The *Oakland Independent* viewed this increase in the African-American population as an indication of potential strength within the community:

> The *Oakland Independent* does not advocate a boycott. That is a weapon unfair, and un-American in principle. The *Independent* advocates and urges the concentrating of our purchasing power.[53]

The irony in the editorial's position is not simply its failure to forecast the economic disaster that loomed ahead, but also its position with regard to boycotts. Within a few short years, both white and black Americans would embrace not only boycotts but also strike activities in an attempt to ameliorate their economic situation in the Great Depression of the 1930s.

The Depression decade marked a watershed in African-American relations with the dominant white society in the East Bay. A new generation of adults, tempered by their experiences in World War I and nurtured under the rhetoric of building a social and political base to wage their campaigns for equity during the 1920s, now faced the need for economic militancy if they were to survive the dislocations forced upon the country by the disaster of economic depression. Although California's total black population comprised only 1.4 percent of the state's inhabitants, it represented 4.3 percent of the California Relief Administration's case load. Afro-Americans on relief comprised 17.8 percent of the state's black population (81,048) by October 1933.[54] The militant posture of African-Americans in California took on aspects not only of willingness to affiliate with unions, such as the BSCP, and wage strike actions, but also to campaign vigorously for political representation. The Unemployment Insurance Act was introduced to California's State Legislature in 1931 and created an unemployment reserve fund to which employers contributed in sums of two percent and employees by one percent of wages paid and earned. The employer collected the money and paid it into the reserve fund.[55] California's African-American families sought public assistance at a rate of four times more than whites and twice the amount of other non-whites.[56]

In the unenviable position of being the first to experience unemployment in most company cutbacks, African-Americans began to rally around the NAACP's national campaign to procure employment in 1931. Worked out by the national office of the NAACP, the campaign consisted of three activities: 1) the appointment of committees to insure that Negroes received their proper share of positions in city departments and municipal, county and state jobs; 2) an inquiry into administrative procedures of local, state, and federal funding for unemployment relief in order to prevent discriminatory practices; and 3) a "Buy Where You Can Work" campaign.[57] Black communities no longer debated the attributes of concentrating their purchasing power as they had done in the 1920s but now clearly welded employment and spending together. Democrat Augustus F. Hawkins of Los Angeles ran for the California Assembly on a platform addressing economic issues in 1934; his success made him the second black legislator for the state of California.[58]

Franklin D. Roosevelt's New Deal programs found many receptive participants among the East Bay's African-American population. Public works projects, such as San Francisco's construction of a psychopathic hospital and cancer institute and a new Third Street Bridge, offered some employment as early as 1931. However, the New Deal extended that employment to black Americans in its massive federal projects which constructed the San Francisco Bay Bridge, the Golden Gate Bridge, the Oakland Airport, Treasure Island, and the Naval Supply Depot and Air Station. The committees of inquiry set forth by the NAACP campaign challenged discriminatory hiring practices which often prevented blacks from receiving work in federal programs.[59] In 1936, C.L. Dellums headed several delegations to the office of Alameda's District Attorney, Earl Warren, arguing for Negro and Jewish representatives in Warren's office. Finally Nathan Henry Miller became Warren's first Jewish assistant.

Persistence also achieved change with regard to discriminatory practices among nurses at Alameda's Highland Training Hospital. Black leaders protested in 1933 against the Alameda Hospital Commission's refusal to allow African-American nurses to room with white, Chinese, and Japanese students at Highland Training Hospital. It was not until 1939, however, that the Alameda County Supervisors ordered that discrimination in the housing of nurses while training be discontinued.[60] Although the Works Progress Administration hired black nurses for public hospitals, such as Highland, during the depression private hospitals did not use black nurses as a rule.[61]

Aware that discrimination existed in employment hiring procedures as well as in housing arrangements, local NAACP members promoted fair employment practices through the local Y.M.C.A. by organizing Civil Service coaching schools. Many African-Americans registered with the Y.M.C.A. in the late 1930s for Civil Service training.[62]

Local vigilance with regard to the administration of New Deal programs remained strong throughout the 1930s in the Oakland Bay Area. In his oral history C.L. Dellums recounted a particular problem which northern Californians had with the National Youth Administration (NYA). Promoting the care of young people, mainly teenagers, the NYA took over Asilomar as a residence center for teenagers from all areas of northern California. There were ample facilities for them to sleep as well as a huge dining room for them. Workshops were set up so that the teenagers could learn vocational skills by which they could earn a living.[63] This center was open to teenagers of all races. However, Mary Bethune petitioned the National Youth Administration to set up Negro Sections for each state. The provision was meant to help Southern blacks achieve equity in the administration of NYA programs in their states. Yet northern and western states had no intention of forming segregated units and did not want them. Dellums and Augustus Hawkins opposed the provision of a Negro Section of the NYA in California and went to Senator Sheridan Downey who convinced Washington to investigate the provision for California. Mike Smith, Senator Downey's aide, came from Washington to Asilomar and then went back to confer with Bethune stating there was no need for segregation in California's National Youth Administration. Bethune asked for further consultation from Dr. O'Hara Lenier (later the first president of Texas Southern University in Houston). Lenier agreed with Smith's assessment and urged the abolition of the Negro Section of the NYA in California.[64]

It took two years, however, to abolish the segregated centers. Because of his protest, Dellums was appointed to serve on a State Advisory Committee to reorganize the California NYA. Through his work on the Asilomar center he met Helen Gahagan Douglas who also served on the committee. Her support for an end to segregated centers enhanced her appeal in the predominantly Negro Central Avenue district of Los Angeles which was part of her constituency.[65] The interracial efforts of these politicians prevented further introduction of segregation to California through New Deal programs.

Economic Militancy

Dellums already faced the segregation of Jim Crow crews—all Negroes—that worked the waterfront on the Grace Line and Luckenbach Steamship docks in 1934.[66] Prior to 1934 African-Americans were restricted from joining organized labor unions along the waterfront. African-Americans in the Bay Area faced the decision whether to affiliate in unions as auxiliary non-voting members during a nation-wide strike wave that began late in 1932 for better wages, better working conditions, and against company-controlled hiring halls. In the Bay Area, dock workers faced an early morning hiring process called "the shape-up" which meant workers had to kick back part of their pay to company representatives in order to receive a good job."[67] During the 1920s and early 1930s, port stewards kept white dock workers "in tow" by offering jobs to African-Americans if the white workers complained about the shape-up. This served to create further antagonism by the white workers toward African-American seamen. In the 1934 San Francisco strike pickets were attacked by police for demanding the right to organize in unions of their choice free from control of company agents and for better wages and control over their working conditions. Members of the Industrial Association of San Francisco, an employers' group that opposed unionization and encouraged open shops, announced they would reopen the waterfront by force. On July 5, 1934, an armed battle broke out along the Embarcadero between strikers and police who tried pushing the strikers back from Pier 38 where strikebreaking trucks were operating. Two of the striking pickets were killed that day when a man emerged from a car and opened fire at the intersection of Mission and Steuart, just around the corner from the International Longshoremen's Association's strike headquarters.[68] Strikers nearby began to mob policemen who were shooting at the crowd attempting to overturn the car in the intersection. Later at a meeting of over 20,000 dock workers in San Francisco's Civic Auditorium where Mayor Rossi and the city's police force were denounced. A mass funeral for the slain workers followed on July 9, 1934, with 40,000 people in attendance. Paul Elier, a staff member of the Industrial Association of San Francisco, summed up the effect of the funeral cortege when he said:

> Its dramatic qualities moved the entire community without regard to individual points of view as to the justice and

righteousness of the striker's cause. It created a temporary but tremendous wave of sympathy for the workers.[69]

Emerging as a rank-and-file leader among workers of the International Longshoremen's Association (ILA), Harry Bridges appealed to the workers directly over the heads of union leaders such as Joseph P. Ryan. The ILA had closed all Pacific Coast ports during the 1934 strike action. Bridges, Australian by birth and witness to the Australian General Strike of 1917, advocated the militancy of a general strike on the West Coast in 1934.[70] On July 17, 1934, an estimated 125,000 people walked off their jobs for three days. The longshoremen wanted $1 an hour, shorter workdays, safer working conditions, and the end of the "shape-up." By October, 1934, the longshoremen received wage increases, improved working conditions, and the right to a hiring hall that assigned jobs without discrimination.

After a long and largely unsuccessful struggle to enter the unions, black workers had to decide in 1934 whether or not to honor the general strike. C.L. Dellums (whose memories of the strike vote which the BSCP had taken in 1928 were still fresh) asked that workers not break the strike. At the time men could join the Longshoremen's Union for $.50 so Dellums handed out fifty-cent pieces during the strike until he could spare no more. Then he asked Bridges to allow African-Americans to sign up for the union and let them pay later. In that fashion, many blacks joined the ILA's picket lines in 1934.[71] Dellums knew that employers encouraged African-Americans to break the strike by working on ships anchored in the middle of the bay. He attended a meeting of strikebreakers where shipowners were rounding up strikebreakers who they would later:

> slip down to the waterfront in the dark and put them in some kind of little boats and take them out to these ships in the middle of the bay and they would live on the ships.[72]

Urging the men not to break the strike, Dellums broke up the meeting of over 150 men. Not all African-Americans approved of the tactic of the general strike. Many well-educated blacks—doctors, lawyers, and school teachers—opposed the unionization of labor and often tried to change the sympathies of laborers' wives and children. As a result Bridges sent teamsters and longshoremen to sit in cars outside the Dellums residence to insure his protection from both disgruntled whites as well as blacks during the 1934 strike.[73] Harry Bridges believed in equality of treatment for blacks and that would become official union policy after the West Coast longshoremen formed the International Longshoremen's and Warehousemen's Union (ILWU) in 1937. However, African-American membership in the ILWU did not become significant until the growth of defense industries on the West Coast during World War II.

Although the San Francisco General Stike resulted in the replacement of the "shape-up" hiring of dock workers with a union-controlled hiring hall, labor's problems on the West Coast did not end in 1934. Two years later in April, 1936, the ultra-radical Pacific Coast Maritime Federation boycotted the Grace liner, *Santa Rosa*, for not carrying a red brand (affiliation with the International Seamen's Union) on their union books. At San Francisco's docks, a committee from the Maritime Federation called on Grace officials to demand that the entire crew be discharged. Suspending relations with the San Francisco Longshoremen's Union, the Grace Line forced the ILA to reverse its stand against the crew of the *Santa Rosa*.[74]

Later that year Angelo Herndon, Negro organizer and Communist labor organizer, spoke to San Francisco's trade unionists and African-American leaders. Herndon became a celebrated labor organizer after leading a biracial relief demonstration to the County Commissioners in Atlanta, Georgia, during the summer of 1932. The demonstration resulted in the commissioners granting an immediate sum of $6000 to the unemployed in the county. It also resulted in Herndon's arrest under an 1861 Georgia law related to the incitement of slave insurrections. Sentenced to serve eighteen to twenty years in prison, Herndon was freed by the U.S. Supreme Court in a decision of five to four on April 26, 1937.[75]

Through the appearances of Herndon in 1936 and Tom Mooney at a mass labor rally of 25,000 people on January 8, 1939, in San Francisco after his release from San Quentin as well as the combined experiences of the strike years, a tentative integration of black workers into the Bay Area labor force.[76]

This integration was not without conflict. The International Brotherhood of Boilermakers and Iron Shipbuilders and Helpers of America, representing seventy percent of all Bay Area shipyard workers, had an all-white union until 1937. At that time it authorized the creation of all-black "auxilliaries" to their existing locals. Auxilliary members paid union dues but had no right to grievance procedures, no business agents to represent them, and no vote on union leadership at any level.[77] Many unions, such as the Culinary Workers International and the International Association of Machinists, had color clauses which stipulated what types of positions blacks could hold. Nevertheless, African-American gains in labor did occur and Dellums's position in favor of the General Strike became widely accepted among blacks in the Bay Area.[78] By the mid-1930s the Alameda County Central Labor Council, a body of various union delegates affiliated with the AFL, seated two African-Americans on the council—Dellums as BSCP delegate and Ishmael Flory as a delegate from the Dining Car Cooks and Waiters Union.[79]

The gubernatorial campaign of 1934 became a focal point for political discontent throughout California, and its issues reflected the economic problems of a nation in depression. At San Francisco's Palace Hotel, Raymond L. Haight, the Commonwealth Progressive candidate, urged that the state "kick the politicians out of office by forcing them to speak the truth in the campaign."[80] Throughout the first part of April Haight's name was combined with Alameda's District Attorney, Earl Warren, as a fusion ticket presenting Haight for Governor and Warren for Attorney General. The "76 Clubs" which promoted this fusion were disappointed when Haight announced on April 25 that he remained a registered Republican who would wage an independent campaign.[81] By June 7 Haight became the gubernatorial candidate of the Commonwealth ticket while Lieutenant Governor Frank Merriam became Governor after James Rolph died in office.

Haight appealed to Republicans telling them they needed new leadership and a progressive program. His program suggested the state be reorganized into five counties instead of fifty-five and endorsed food distribution by ending the Agricultural Adjustment Act's destruction of food surpluses in the state. Establishing New Leadership Clubs throughout the state, Haight campaigned for farm relief by tax reduction, a Central Valley water project, and the establishment of a Department of State to aid co-operative unemployed groups.[82] Haight blamed the San Francisco General Strike on Governor Merriam, Communist organizers, and popular apathy. This progressive reform approach to the labor problems of the day was countered by Upton Sinclair's End Poverty in California (EPIC) campaign. Although Franklin Roosevelt failed to endorse Sinclair's Democratic bid for election, Sinclair did attract more Bay Area blacks to his platform than did Haight or Merriam. Election totals for Oakland's Thirteenth Assembly District gave Sinclair 13,648 votes, a narrow margin over Merriam's 13,087 votes. The election totals for Oakland's Fifteenth Assembly District also gave Sinclair a narrow margin of 12,959 votes to Merriam's 12,770 votes. The election precincts of West Oakland which were heavily populated with African-American residents helped give Sinclair his narrow margin of victory over Merriam in the Thirteenth and Fifteenth Assembly Districts.[83] Clearly African-Americans by 1934 identified poverty as the major issue facing them and were willing to step away from mainstream political candidates in order to resolve its problems.

Aware of the importance of the political process for bringing about community goals, Frances Albrier decided to run for Berkeley's City Council in 1939:

> We women hadn't become very active in politics. They knew something about it, but they weren't active in running for offices. But, I knew that I didn't file or run to be elected—I didn't think I would *be* elected, because I didn't think that people were broadminded enough to elect a black woman. But I was in for a surprise. I received a great many votes. My idea of running was to meet the people. I knew that if I ran for city council, I would be invited to the clubs and organizations to give my views of the city government. I wanted to tell them that we had 5,000 taxpayers without *any* representation in the city government or the schools of Berkeley. That was the message I wanted to get over to them because later we had planned to make an issue.[84]

The *San Francisco News* and the *Berkeley Gazette* carried articles describing Albrier's character and ability. John D. Barry, one of the reporters who viewed Albrier's candidacy favorably, wrote that:

> Something quite interesting is happening in Berkeley. There's a colored woman running for the City Council. We don't often hear of a colored woman running for any office. Surely we don't hear of it in this part of the world.[85]

Although she did not win the election, Albrier's campaign proved quite credible and offered her the community recognition which she needed in future campaigns.

During the latter part of the depression decade Frances Albrier volunteered for community work throughout the East Bay. Her base of support became the numerous and overlapping mutual aid organizations she either belonged to or created. Elected the first female member of the Alameda County Democratic Central Committee in 1938, Albrier quickly recognized the need for African Americans to use the political process to their advantage within urban-based communities outside of the American South.[86]

As manager of the East Bay Democratic Campaign Headquarters for the election of state officials in 1938, Albrier used her position to pressure community, state, and federal programs to support employment for African Americans. In 1939 after writing to Robert C. Schnitzer, Supervisor of the Federal Theatre Project at Treasure Island, Albrier helped secure W.P.A. jobs for the Keeton Chorus musicians scheduled to play the "Swing Mikado" at the Golden Gate International Exposition. The W.P.A. had considered decreasing the thirty positions reserved for the Keeton Chorus but decided to maintain all positions after Albrier's protest.[87]

During 1939 and 1940 Frances Albrier helped organize both the Citizen's Employment Council and the East Bay Women's Welfare Club, groups seeking the economic and educational integration of the East Bay's black population with the dominant white population. In a "Don't Buy Where You Can't Work" campaign, the Citizen's Employment Council picketed Mr. King's Sacramento Market in Berkeley so that the store owner would hire African American clerks. Observing that some black women failed to honor the picket line, Frances Albrier wrote the following article published in the Citizen's Employment Council *Bulletin* during the picketing:

> From observation and checking of those of our Group who disregarded the picket line, we found that women were in the majority.

> It was quite regrettable. The future of the race lies within its women. A race cannot rise any higher than its women will allow it. The Negro woman has a very great responsibility. She of all persons should be loyal to her race; and in her heart should be the two slogans: loyal to her God; loyal to her Race.[88]

The campaign ended when Mr. King hired the first two African American clerks to work in the Sacramento Market in the spring of 1940. The Citizen's Employment Council received aid from the Angus Club, a men's social club in Oakland, as well as the East Bay Women's Welfare Club.

While working on the campaign for employment integration at Sacramento Market, East Bay mothers began to explore the possibility of hiring African Americans as teachers in the Berkeley public school system. Beginning in September 1939, Berkeley's African American women mounted a five year campaign to hire the first black teacher in Berkeley's public schools. Members of the East Bay Women's Welfare Club kept presenting their desire for an African American teacher in the Berkeley schools to Dr. Dickson, Superintendent of Schools, and to the Berkeley School Board. Every year, Dr. Dickson would tell the women that he "was working on it." Dickson gradually prepared Longfellow Schools for its first African American teacher by removing from Longfellow a principal and some white teachers opposed to integration, leaving a position open in the kindergarten.[89] By 1943 Dr. Dickson hired Ruty Acty as Longfellow's first African American kindergarten teacher. Acty later remarked that she thought:

> one of the reasons they put her into kindergarten was because kindergarten was not a requirement in the school district at that time. If white parents objected to having their children in the class with her, they could remove them.[90]

However, employment opportunities were not the only grievance of East Bay African Americans. As a result of the great migration of African-Americans during the 1920s from southern communities to the north and west, Bay Area residents found housing difficult to buy and most African-Americans remained tenants. However, even housing rentals were scarce and the competition for them increased in the 1930s. In West and North competition for them increased in the 1930s. In West and North Oakland the increasing need for housing was temporarily assuaged by homeowners and tenants taking in boarders. Blacks confronted the lack of available housing and restrictive ordinances based on race by organizing neighborhood improvement associations and by campaigning for equitable housing laws. The *California Voice* reported in 1922 that a "small number of Berkeley residents [were] trying to pass an ordinance that would prohibit the members of our group owning homes in the district."[91] Several restrictive ordinances did pass, however. Wall's Addition to the city of Richmond advertised that restrictive housing covenants existed in Lakeshore Glen, South Lakeshore Glen, and Lakeshore Hills:

> Savages running wild in a central African forest, living on wild nuts and fruit, sleeping in trees or caves, don't care much about a home—they don't want property because they can't take care of it. But white men, civilized men, twentieth century Americans, should need no argument to make them see the beauty of owning property-real property—A HOME.[92]

The NAACP tried to break restrictions as well as encourage employment for blacks with regard to housing construction. In 1938 an NAACP committee inquired why so few Negroes were used in the building trades only to find that most of the trades union had color restrictions.[93] Not only was it hard to find employment working on new housing projects, but restrictions also existed excluding blacks from the projects constructed by the Federal Housing Administration. Sheffield Village, constructed by the FHA, had a restrictive clause stating "For use only by persons whose blood is entirely of the Caucasian race, except strictly in the capacity of domestic servants."[94]

Oakland could participate in low-cost housing by adopting an enabling resolution to participate and then set up the Housing Authority to work on it in New Deal days. The federal law provided a local municipality could get in on the program by adopting a motion, a resolution on its own volition. A city would have to consider it upon a petition signed by a certain number of local residents—very small number of signatures—something like twenty-five.[95] The Oakland City Council would not consider an enabling resolution so Dellums started to lead demonstrations in city council meetings through Labor's Non-Partisan League. The City Hall housed the jail and Negroes didn't like to go there; hence, Dellums used the Labor League.[96] The Oakland League of Women Voters backed low-cost housing and spoke for it. At least 90 percent of the people demonstrating in city council meetings were white.[97] When the resolution was passed, two businessmen (one dealing in downtown business properties and only residential properties in Piedmont) were placed on the Housing Authority. They appraised houses, according to Dellums, while sitting in their cars—never going indoors. Then they sent to Washington a very low evaluation for West Oakland which was cut down by 40 percent by Washington. People refused to sell for such low prices and the Housing Authority realtor came looking for Dellums to help. He got Washington to reexamine the appraisals and increase the price so that it was no longer a steal. However, no one felt they received a "fair" price for their home. Some held out until they went to court.[98]

The second phase of the low-cost housing fight was deciding policy for selecting tenants. Blacks demanded that the Oakland Housing Authority announce a public policy of integration but the Housing Authority would not comply. Instead it opened Campbell Village and selected William P. Butler, an African-American realtor and friend of Dellums, to manage it. Butler selected tenants to checkerboard the Village:

> It became a showplace of the nation for public housing projects. He checkerboarded every floor, every unit, and it lasted for years that way and the people got along just beautifully.[99]

Tensions subsided after Campbell Village was built. The next housing project—Peralta—had integrated segregation:

> One building would be all-white, the next building all-Negro. But there was no integration in the buildings, no checkerboarding, in various buildings. This is what we called integrated segregation.[100]

The third project—Lockwood—was all-white when it first opened. "You see how they went? From integration to integrated segregation to lily-whiteism."[101] Eventually Peralta had Butler as a manager but it was really too late for change there. Lockwood was in East Oakland which was predominantly white. Negroes lived beyond Lockwood in East Oakland all the way out to 90th Avenue.[102]

Adequate housing for African-Americans living in the East Bay continued to deteriorate until it became a recognized crisis during World War II. However, the campaigns for federal and local housing aid created an increased awareness that consistent pressure groups were necessary to promote African-American goals in the Bay Area. The Negro Educational Council of the East Bay, a group of ten people, organized in 1935 to sponsor a radio show, *Negroes in the News*. The council believed that a weekly radio program on station KLS would help offset the lack of news regarding the African-American community in the East Bay. The radio program was supported by Stuart Warner, employed at Warner Brothers' Studios, and the owners of radio station, KLS.[103] Throughout the 1920s and 1930s African-Americans consistently sought avenues for creating political and economic voice in the larger white-dominated community of California's East Bay. World War II hastened this search by changing the African-American focus upon integration through community building efforts to a more militant political stance.

NOTES

1. *California Voice*, 7 January 1922, p. 2.
2. *Ibid.*, p. 1.
3. Department of Justice, Bureau of Investigation, *Federal Surveillance of Black Americans, 1916-1925*. Records Relating to the UNIA, San Francisco, Office of Naval Intelligence, Confidential Correspondence, 1913-1924. Casefile 20964-2194-L [Washington D.C.: National Archives and Records Administration, RG38], 00700, microfilm. Another account of this episode is given in *The Marcus Garvey and Universal Negro Improvement Association Papers* which contain a report, from J.J. Hannigan, Commander, U.S. Navy Intelligence Officer, to the Director of the Office of Naval Intelligence. Hannigan stated that the "These detectives sneaked in. They threatened that in case Mr. Garvey would say a word that would lead to political and racial instigation, he would be arrested. But Garvey did not care, and the detectives would/not/find any fault with what he had to say." J.J. Hannigan, to the Director, Office of Naval Intelligence (12 June 1922), "Universal Negro Improvement Association," in *The Marcus Garvey and Universal Negro Improvement Association Papers* (Berkeley and Los Angeles: The University of California Press, 1985), 669-672.
4. Crouchett, Bunch, and Winnacker, *Visions Toward Tomorrow*, 33.
5. Malca Chall, *Determined Advocate for Racial Equality* (Berkeley, CA: Regional Oral History Office, Bancroft Library, 1977-78): 69.
6. For an account of Delilah Beasley's activities during the 1920s, see *The Oakland Independent*, 14 December 1929, p. 1; Delilah L. Beasley, *The Negro Trail Blazers of California* (Los Angeles: 1919; repr. San Francisco: R and E Research Associates, 1968).
7. *California Voice*, 18 April 1930, p. 1.
8. Crouchett, Bunch, and Winnacker, *Visions Toward Tomorrow*, 29. Dr. Crouchett discussed the persistence of black students trying to fully integrate campus life as late as the period from 1948-1951 when they mounted a campaign for integrated housing in campus dormitories. Dr. Lawrence Crouchett, interview by author, Telephone conversation, Oakland, California, 3 August 1989.

9. Since the use of "Cal" remains a popular colloquialism for the University of California, Berkeley, I will refer to Cal when discussing student affairs and sports at the University.

10. Several primary sources exist for Walter Gordon's biography and contributions to civil rights actions in the East Bay. Several tape-recorded interviews with Gordon's contemporaries exist as part of the Earl Warren Oral History Project. See Joyce Henderson, *C.L. Dellums: International President of the Brotherhood of Sleeping Car Porters and Civil Rights Leader* (Berkeley, California: Regional Oral History Office, Bancroft Library, 1973); Henderson, *Tarea Hall Pittman*; and Joyce A. Henderson, Amelia Fry and Edward France, *William Byron Rumford: Legislator for Fair Employment, Fair Housing, and Public Health* (Berkeley, California: Regional Oral History Office, Bancroft Library, 1973). See also Crouchett, Bunch, and Winnacker, *Visions Toward Tomorrow*, 26-27.

11. Henderson, *C.L. Dellums*, 93.

12. The exclusion of African-American students from the University of California's dormitories in Berkeley lasted until the early 1950s when black student leaders began to press for integration. Nathan Irvin Huggins (1927-1989), noted historian and author of *Harlem Renaissance* and *Black Odyssey*, remembered attending the University of California, Berkeley, on the GI Bill after World War II. He became a leader in the Associated Student Body "because Berkeley was so large, they didn't know what color I was until they got to know who I was, and by then I had established a track record." Leon Litwack, "Obituary: Nathan Irvin Huggins," *OAH Newsletter* (February, 1990), 5.

13. Henderson, *Tarea Hall Pittman*, 98.

14. Irving Stone chronicled Rumford's college days in *There Was Light* (New York, 1970).

13Joyce A. Henderson, Amelia Fry and Edward France, *William Byron Rumford: Legislator for Fair Employment, Fair Housing, and Public Health*, (Berkeley, California: Regional Oral History Office, Bancroft Library, 1973), 24.

16. *California Voice*, 1 October 1921, p. 1.

17. Henderson, *C.L. Dellums*, 91.

18. *California Voice*, 1 October 1921, p. 1.

19. Henderson, *C.L. Dellums*, 89.

20. *California Voice*, 15 December 1925, p. 1.

21. *Oakland Western American*, 28 May 1926, p. 1.; *Oakland Western American*, 6 August 1926, p. 1.
22. Henderson, *Tarea Hall Pittman*, 50.
23. *Ibid.*, 51-52.
24. *Ibid.*, 52.
25. *Oakland Times*, 29 September 1933, p. 1.
26. *Ibid.*, p. 1.
27. The African-American press covered community sports affairs faithfully throughout the decades, 1920-1940. *California Voice*, 14 October 1938, p.1; *Oakland Western American*, 28 May 1926, p. 7; *Ibid.*, 6 August 1926, p. 5; *Oakland Times*, 29 September 1933.
28. In the case of the white primary, the Supreme Court in *Nixon v. Herndon*, 273 U.S. 536, used the Fourteenth Amendment to say white primaries were unconstitutional because they denied equal protection of the laws. The Texas legislature ignored this ruling by authorizing any party's state executive committee to prescribe qualifications for membership; meanwhile the Democratic executive committee resolved to limit membership to whites. In *Nixon v. Condon*, 286 U.S. 73, the Supreme Court again found denial of equal protection of the laws. However, in 1935, the Supreme Court found that the Democratic party *as a private organization* could bar Negroes from its primaries (*Grovey v. Townsend*, 295 U.S. 45). Brainerd Dyer, "One Hundred Years of Negro Suffrage," 14.
29. Vincent Gordon Harding, "Wrestling Toward the Dawn: The Afro-American Freedom Movement and the Changing Constitution," *The Journal of American History* 74 (December 1987): 728.
30. Henderson, *C.L. Dellums*, 3.
31. *Ibid.*, 4.
32. *Oakland Western American*, 24 September 1926, 4.
33. Henderson, *C.L. Dellums*, 6.
34. Prince Hall Masons began when an African-American, Prince Hall, went to England after the American Revolution to receive a charter to organize Masonry for African-Americans in the United States since white Masonic groups would not admit them. *Ibid.*, 9-12.
35. *Ibid.*, 14.
36. *Ibid.*, 19.

37. Although the Pullman Company did not recognize the BSCP, Dellums forced the local company officials to deal with him. *Ibid.*, 16-17.

38. The Brotherhood of Sleeping Car Porters was first organized in Harlem, New York, in order to deal with a long list of grievances by Pullman porters. When A. Philip Randolph agreed to become general organizer of the BSCP, his magazine, *The Messenger*, became the voice of the brotherhood. It is not surprising that Dellums, an avid reader of *The Messenger*, would be among the first Pullman porters on the West Coast to join the BSCP. Jervis Anderson, *A. Philip Randolph: A Biographical Portrait* (New York: Harcourt Brace Jovanovich, Inc., 1972), 5.

39. Henderson, *C.L. Dellums*, 25.

40. The *Chicago Whip* and the *Chicago Defender* advised that Pullman porters should support the Company's Employee Representation Plan. The plan was basically an extension of Pullman's Personnel Department and went so far as to finance elections of representatives to the "company union." Philip S. Foner and Ronald L. Lewis, eds., *The Era of Post-War Prosperity and the Great Depression, 1920-1936*, vol 6, *The Black Worker: A Documentary History from Colonial Times to the Present* (Philadelphia: Temple University Press, 1981), 190.

41. Henderson, *C.L. Dellums*, 25, 30. The railroad workers employed in Oakland included Pullman porters, cooks, waiters, redcaps, baggage-handlers, railyard laborers and maids employed by Southern Pacific, and the Santa Fe and Pullman yards in Richmond. Crouchett, Bunch, and Winnacker, *Visions Toward Tomorrow*, 68.

42. Henderson, *C.L. Dellums*, 28-29.

43. *Ibid.*, 35.

44. *Ibid.*, 45.

45. A. Philip Randolph outlined the meaning of a strike vote in his article, "Our Next Step," which he wrote for *The Messenger* in April 1928. Foner and Lewis, *The Era of Post-War Prosperity*, 265.

46. A letter from Milton P. Webster (Chicago Division Organizer for the BSCP) and Dad Moore (organizer for the Oakland porters), June 25, 1928, responded to Moore's fear that Communist party members were advising the Oakland porters on strike activities. A subsequent letter to Webster from A. Philip Randolph, June 27, 1928, confirmed that Webster had indicated to Randolph the situation in Oakland as he had learned of it from

Dad Moore. Randolph thanked Webster for "informing me of the nefarious activities of the Communists in Oakland, California." He indicated that he sent air mail letters to Brothers Dad Moore and C.L. Dellums to warn that the BSCP "cannot temporize with this Communist menace. It's a sinister and destructive crowd which will stop at nothing in order to realize its aim which is to wreck and ruin every organization which is not Communistic." Randolph believed that the Pullman Company could even be financing the Communist workers in order to discredit the BSCP. Foner and Lewis, *The Era of Post-War Prosperity*, 289-290. For an account of the role played by Dellums, see Henderson, *C.L. Dellums*, 65.

47. *Ibid.*, 48-50.

48. *Ibid.*, 53.

49. There were seven vice-presidents elected by region. Frank Boyd of St. Paul, Minnesota, was first nominated against Dellums, but Boyd announced that it was silly to nominate him for the Pacific Coast region. George Clark, a realtor from Los Angeles, was nominated only to decline when Randolph told him that he couldn't guarantee a salary and preferred Dellums anyway. After a recess, Lonnie Hampton from Fort Worth, Texas, ran unsuccessfully against Dellums. *Ibid.*, 40-41.

50. *Ibid.*, 55.

51. Chall, 76.

52. The *Chicago Whip* published a survey showing that more than 50 percent of the businesses that blacks frequented did not hire blacks. The *Whip* found that Afro-American civic organizations, such as Women's Clubs, Business Leagues, lodges, and churches, took heed. They began to urge concentration of buying power at only those businesses which employed Afro-Americans. *Oakland Independent*, 19 October 1929, 8.

53. *Ibid.*

54. Roger Olmsted and Charles Wollenberg, eds., *Neither Separate nor Equal: Race and Racism in California* (San Francisco: California Historical Society, 1971), ??

55. *San Francisco Labor Clarion*, 30 January 1931, 1.

56. Crouchett, Bunch, and Winnacker, *Visions Toward Tomorrow*, 35.

57. The slogan "Don't Buy Where You Can't Work" was first introduced by the Urban League in New York in 1929. *San Francisco Labor Clarion*, 26 November 1931, 7.

58. James A. Fisher suggests that the victory of Assemblyman Hawkins indicated "that blacks in California were ready for a new deal. By the middle of the 1930s, California's estimated 57,000 black voters had heeded the popular axiom: 'Lincoln freed us, and Roosevelt feeds us.'" Fisher, "The Political Development of the Black Community," 41.

59. Crouchett, Bunch, and Winnacker, *Visions Toward Tomorrow*, 43.

60. *California Voice*, 6 January 1939, 1.

61. Chall, 73-75.

62. *California Voice*, 13 January 1939, 1.

63. Henderson, *C.L. Dellums*, 75.

64. *Ibid.*, 78-79.

65. *Ibid.*, 82.

66. *Ibid.*, 139.

67. The shape-up hiring process involved port stewards representing the companies picking the men they wanted to work on the docks each day. The shape-up became an opportunity for corruption in that the port stewards expected a kickback from their hires. It also put the company in a position to keep the laborers separate by competing with each other. Harvey Schwartz, "Harry Bridges and the Scholars Looking at History's Verdict," *California History* 59 (Spring 1980): 67.

68. The slain men were Howard S. Sperry, a longhoreman, and Nick Counderakis, a cook, known in the Communist Party as Nick Bordoise. David F. Selvin, "Days of Rage," San Francisco *Chronicle*, 3 July 1988, A13-14.

69. *Ibid.*, 13.

70. Immediately after the mass funeral in San Francisco, Bridges received stinging denunciation at the hands of General Hugh S. Johnson who spoke at the Hollywood Bowl characterizing Bridges as a person who did "not even [have] the simple dignity of American citizenship." William F. Dunne, *The Great San Francisco General Strike; The Story of the West Coast Strike-the Bay Counties General Strike and the Maritime Workers Strike*. (New York: Workers Library, 1934): 89.

71. Henderson, *C.L. Dellums*, 136-138.

72. *Ibid.*, 136-137.

73. Dellums derisively called these professional Negroes the "parlor stool pigeon brigade." *Ibid.*, 26, 136.

74. *Seamen's Journal*, 1 May 1936, 1.

75. Foner and Lewis, *The Era of Post-War Prosperity*, 384, 502-503. In addition to his protest of welfare relief cuts, Angelo Herndon went to Atlanta in 1932 as a member of the Communist party with two other missions. Herndon was to organize African-American support for the Communist presidential nominees-William Zebulon Foster and his black running mate, James W. Ford. He was to publicize the Scottsboro case as it went to the U.S. Supreme Court. John Herbert Roper, *C. Vann Woodward, Southerner* (Athens, GA and London: The University of Georgia Press, 1987), 55.

76. Dellums believed Mooney innocent of charges brought against him in the celebrated San Francisco Preparedness Day bombing of July 22, 1916, and worked to get Mooney out of prison. Henderson, *C.L. Dellums*, 61. Immediately after Governor Culbert L. Olson's inaugural address on January 2, 1939, he received a group headed by Mooney's defense attorney, George Davis, Assemblyman Paul Richie, and union leader, Harry Bridges, who presented a formal application for Mooney's pardon. He was formally pardoned by Governor Olson five days later. Richard H. Frost, *The Mooney Case* (Stanford: Stanford University Press, 1968), 483-485.

77. "Explorations in Black Maritime History Exhibit," *Maritime Humanities Newsletter* 2 (Spring 1983): 2, 5.

78. Crouchett, Bunch, and Winnacker, *Visions Toward Tomorrow*, 37.

79. Henderson, *C.L. Dellums*, 57-58.

80. Bob Barger, "Raymond L. Haight and the Commonwealth Progessive Campaign of 1934," *California Historical Society Quarterly* 63 (September 1964): 220-221.

81. *Oakland Tribune*, 25 April 1934, 1.

82. Barger, "Raymond L. Haight and the Commonwealth Progessive Campaign," 223.

83. Secretary of State, State of California, *Certified Abstract of the Statement of the Vote Polled in Alameda County, California, Relating to Votes Given for Governor and Lieutenant Governor, at the General Election, November, 1934* (Sacramento: California State Archives, 1934).

84. Chall, 106.

85. John D. Barry, "Ways of the World," *San Francisco News* (29 April 1939).

86. In his analysis of the civil rights movement, author and political analyst, Doug McAdams, explains that African Americans, through the use of the electoral system and mass action in northern cities, substantially weakened the structural roots of racism. Doug McAdam, *Political Process and the Development of Black Insurgency 1930-1970* (Chicago: University of Chicago Press, 1982).

87. Frances Mary Albrier, Correspondence and Papers (Regional Oral History Office: The Bancroft Library, University of California, Berkeley): Scrapbook.

88. Frances Albrier, "Women," *Citizen's Employment Council Bulletin*, 1940.

89. The percentage of African American children at Longfellow School in 1938 was approximately fifty percent.

90. Chall, 113.

91. *California Voice*, 7 January 1922, 2.

92. *Wall's Addition to the City of Richmond*, Pamphlet 4599-45 [on exhibit at Oakland Northern California Center for Afro-American History and Life].

93. *California Voice*, 28 October 1938, 1.

94. *Restrictions by Federal Housing Administration for Sheffield Village*, 10 March 1939 [on exhibit at Oakland Museum, February 1989].

95. Henderson, *C.L. Dellums*, 26, 67.

96. *Ibid.*, 26, 67.

97. *Ibid.*, 26, 68.

98. *Ibid.*, 26, 69-70.

99. *Ibid.*, 26, 70.

100. *Ibid.*, 26, 72.

101. *Ibid.*, 26, 73.

102. *Ibid.*, 26, 74.

103. Henderson, *Tarea Hall Pittman*, 79.

CHAPTER IV

CATALYST FOR CHANGE:
WARTIME IN CALIFORNIA'S EAST BAY

Although African-Americans often confronted the dichotomy of the California Dream by mounting their own economic and political campaigns during the 1920s and 1930s, the intervention of World War II triggered an increased awareness among black residents of California's East Bay of discriminatory housing and labor policies. The wartime defense industries located in the Bay Area acted as magnets to draw racial and ethnic minorities discouraged by the lack of employment opportunities elsewhere in the country. The East Bay's swollen African-American population during World War II quickly recognized the experienced leadership and programs promoted by black residents for self-help and racial equality during the 1930s.[1] New migrants soon found allies in the African-American activists already living in the Bay Area.

Housing which had always been inadequate for the black community in the Bay Area became a paramount problem during the 1940s. San Francisco and the East Bay finally experienced the "Chicago effect" which Allan Spear noted in his urban study of *Black Chicago*. Spear explained that when the black population is small, the white population does not fear it; but, when numbers increase, conflict occurs. Citing the black population of Chicago as a very small component (0.9 percent) of its total population in 1860, Spear found an absence of racial conflict. However, when the black population increased in Chicago during the next two decades, the white antagonism toward African-Americans surfaced in discriminatory patterns affecting housing and employment.[2] As more African-Americans came to the Bay Area after 1941 patterns of residential segregation increased with the use of occupancy clauses in deeds and leases that restricted racial minorities to certain areas of Oakland and the East Bay. This "Chicago effect" continued to deny equal opportunity in housing to African-Americans long after the war had ended. In 1960 Tarea Hall Pittman, then acting director of the NAACP's West Coast Regional Office, gave testimony to the United States Commission on Civil Rights that "residential segregation based on race is the general rule in the towns and cities in the West."[3]

Prior to World War II, African-Americans made up no more than three percent of the West Coast's shipbuilding industries at most. By 1945 there were more than 700,000 workers in West Coast yards with approximately seven percent (50,000 people) comprised of African-Americans.[4] Nearly thirteen percent of the total workers among the four leading shipbuilding companies of the Bay Area were African-Americans by 1943. People seeking work could apply to the four shipyards of Henry J. Kaiser in Richmond, to Marinship in Sausalito, to the Moore yards in Oakland, or to the Todd yard in San Francisco.

Many black families from the Dustbowl states of the Southwest began to migrate to the Oakland area soon after the war began. Edward L. Coleman, a young African-American migrant to Alameda in 1943, said that a carload of men left his home in El Dorado, Arkansas, every week for California. Coleman's father went with one of the carloads at the urging of his wife who saw the shipyard checks her neighbors' husbands sent home from their jobs in California.[5] The first money order which Coleman's father sent to his wife after a week away from home was clipped on the side showing a denomination of $100. It represented an incredible sum since the Colemans had never been able to earn that much in one week in Arkansas. In El Dorado, Mr. Coleman was a barber and his wife worked in a cleaners. Together they would earn between seventeen and eighteen dollars for a six-day work week.

The high wage rate in the West Coast defense industries drew even reluctant migrants to California. Coleman called his father "the ultimate pessimist" since the senior Coleman believed that the war would not last long enough for the men with whom he left El Dorado to find good jobs in the defense industries. Sometimes it would be six months to a year and a half later when the rest of the family followed the men who went West. The Coleman family came to Oakland in 1943 with no furniture and only their bags and the clothes on their backs. When they arrived in St. Louis en route to California, they found the typical pattern of wartime transportation.

There was mass confusion boarding trains that often were delayed. Railway passengers were segregated; however, Coleman recalls that the segregation did not mean a thing since they were packed with soldiers and there were no seats left for black people. Coleman with his mother and sister stood up in the vestibule of the train and in the toilets practically all the way to Salt Lake City. He remembers his mother going to the bathroom just so she could sit down.[6]

Once the Colemans arrived in Oakland they faced the same housing shortages that other black families found in the Bay Area. They lived for nine months in a housing project where six people lived in a one-bedroom apartment. Tarea Hall Pittman worked for the Richmond Travelers Aid Society, USO, during the war and remembered working with transients and people who were moving into California:

> We had a time opening up the Kaiser Industries, and we had a doubly hard time in trying to get some housing for those men. Some of the people were sleeping in "hot beds." So naturally, when their families came, you'd have a very difficult time finding them because all the landlady knew was that she had a stream of people going and coming. One man would work one shift and sleep in the "hot bed," then that one would be up and gone, and there would be another shift.[7]

California had a three-year residency requirement for public assistance in effect during World War II; however, southern states such as Oklahoma, Texas, and Louisiana—had one-year residency requirements. This meant that people coming to California would lose their former residency while not qualifying for resident status in California. The migration of African-Americans to the wartime defense industries reached staggering proportions by 1945 when approximately 152,000 blacks moved to the West Coast.[8]

Dealing with the needs of migrants rapidly settling in the Bay Area posed special problems for the community. Robert E. Colbert noted in 1946 that:

> So sudden was the deluge that not only was the majority group made conscious of this alien element, but the older Negro residents in this area were probably for the first time made aware of their place as a minority group. Thus was created a problem. Relationships between older Negro residents and whites changed.

Many reactions by these older residents toward the newcomers—the sharecroppers—were experienced.[9]

Assuming that World War II represented a "watershed" in African-American experience, comments such as Colbert's indicated to many that the black community splintered politically between older and more recent residents. This did not occur in California's East Bay where the black "pioneer urbanites" joined forces with the migrant newcomers in order to promote nondiscriminatory policies.[10] For example, the East Bay community of Richmond transformed itself dramatically during World War II while Tarea Pittman worked there for the Travelers Aid Society. From a population of twenty-three thousand people living in one-family houses before the war, Richmond's population grew to over one hundred thousand due to the construction of four Kaiser shipyards and a prefabrication plant built on its waterfront. Activists such as Tarea Pittman as well as local African-American organizations united to monitor the housing and employment conditions of the shipyards throughout the war. Sprawling public-housing projects were built beside the harbor and town of Richmond to accommodate the new shipyard workers who built one-fifth of all the Liberty ships constructed during the war. Shipyard workers in Richmond were drawn by the promise of a high wage which averaged $61 a week. If a worker were lucky enough to find a three-room apartment in someone's private house, he would pay $120 a month for it—almost half his monthly wage.[11] By 1945 there were 14,000 African-Americans in Richmond where fewer than 250 lived before 1940.

Richmond's acute housing shortage and sub-standard construction predated America's entry in the war by several years. The 1940 census reported that out of a total of 7,611 dwellings, 1,539 needed major repairs or had no private bath.[12] On January 21, 1941, the *Oakland Tribune* reported that Richmond's City Council adopted a resolution that formed a five-man housing authority to investigate "unsafe, unsanitary and congested dwelling accommodations."[13] The housing authority was charged with making a city-wide survey and report of housing units in the city of Richmond in order to initiate action designed to request the construction of low-cost housing units from the United States

Housing Authority. The resolution passed by the Richmond City Council in January, 1941, claimed that:

> Unemployment and the existence of unsafe, unsanitary and congested dwelling accommodations have produced an alarming economic and social condition. Emergency measures are necessary for the immediate preservation of public peace, health and safety.[14]

Council members expressed concern about the expected influx of workers who would seek housing in Richmond later in the year after the Todd-California shipyard in San Francisco began its full production schedule. Many shipyard workers, unable to find housing in San Francisco, would commute by ferry from Richmond to their work at the Todd Shipyard. By the end of 1941 two low-cost housing projects were completed; however, neither project admitted African-Americans although most of Richmond's black population would have qualified for low-income housing.

Three years later many of the newly constructed shipyard housing units built in Richmond with the aid of the federal government failed to pass an inquest held by the Contra Costa county coroner's jury. In January, 1944, eight unidentified African-American shipyard workers were killed in a fire at Dormitory "O", located at South 11th Street and Potrero Avenue. Richmond's fire chief, William P. Cooper, testified before the coroner's jury that various Richmond housing units were "totally unsafe, and built in violation of all state, local and national laws."[15] Of the 24,000 housing units built during the war, only 750 were permanent dwellings with the majority of African-Americans in Richmond living in the temporary housing units. Cooper also testifed that the Richmond Housing Authority was not to blame for the unsafe conditions. The FSA, the PWA, the FHA and other governmental agencies built the units and turned them over to the housing authority to administer. Cooper said:

> I've written to the various authorities and commissions telling them about conditions in these housing units. I've told them they are unsafe. I've told them they are endangering the lives of shipyard workers and their families. I've pleaded with them to

remedy the situation—I've ordered them to take steps to remedy these conditions. And they've told me to go to hell![16]

A survey following the January, 1944, fire showed that of 9000 units housing between 50,000 and 90,000 persons only 64 had fire protection including alarm systems and fire hydrants. Cooper revealed that in one section of the housing projects, fire hydrants were installed but were not turned on for three months as "none of the agencies knew which one had the authority to order the water turned on."[17]

The alarm caused by the hazards of inadequate fire protection in Richmond's shipyard housing exacerbated tensions already present among the city's African-American community. Representatives of local black organizations complained of illegal evictions and threatened a "rent strike" if the evictions did not cease.

The city council recommended that the Housing Authority establish a definite policy concerning evictions and illegal tenancy. Charles Strothoff, executive secretary for the Richmond Housing Authority, released its policies and procedures to the public on January 21, 1944. The definition of eligibility for housing authority units and rooms included those persons working in certain war industries. The names of the war industries were not disclosed by Strothoff. Strothoff said complaints of illegal tenancy occurred when families moved into housing units without acceptance of a formal application:

> Legal residents all must have signed leased with the authority. In cases of evictions for non-payment of rent, the authority must, and will, follow State and O.P.A. rules and regulations. . . . In cases where families are illegally occupying a unit, each case will be handled separately and those families who are working in eligible war industries [we] will try to place the families as rapidly as possible.[18]

Four years later Richmond's housing crisis still went unresolved as the city's Chamber of Commerce declared a section of north Richmond a "blighted area" that was "hazardous to health and the public welfare."[19] African-Americans charged that the area's designation as "blighted" was an attempt by the city of Richmond to acquire more land at cheap prices for industrial development.

Opposition by the white community in Richmond to the expansion of African-American residential areas followed the patterns and tactics used throughout the San Francisco Bay area: 1) real estate agents and home owners refused to sell property to African-Americans; 2) restrictive covenants were employed despite legal pronouncements against them; 3) banks and other lending institutions either refused to make loans to African-Americans or else they scrutinized minority applications so stringently that few succeeded; and 4) occupancy criteria maintaining the previous racial composition of "neighborhoods" were upheld by government agencies that built new residential units or financed housing.[20] A Real Property Survey taken for Oakland in 1936 showed very few African-American residents in the Oakland-Berkeley hills region. The survey stated that restrictive covenants were partially behind this *de facto* segregation.[21] The heavily concentrated African-American district of West Oakland attracted more industrial than residential growth and thereby increased the housing shortage for black residents of Oakland. By 1938 a series of studies to determine the need for low-cost housing verified that Oakland did have substandard housing conditions and could qualify for federal funding. The studies recommended that areas in West Oakland should be demolished. The first projects were proposed for the heart of West Oakland—areas bounded by 8th-12th-Cypress-Union and Poplar streets and by 8th-10th-Campbell and Willow streets. African-Americans residing in West Oakland used a community relocation service to find new homes in North Oakland and South Berkeley. By July, 1941, the first of the new low-cost housing projects opened in West Oakland with a total of 154 units distributed according to the racial patterns found in the neighborhood before construction began. The new project, Campbell Village, housed approximately 57 percent African-American residents to 41 percent white residents. Although black and white families lived on the same floors in Campbell Village, this "checkerboard pattern" would not be followed in other wartime housing projects throughout the East Bay. Other housing projects would either have non-whites reside in separate buildings or in separate projects entirely.

The city of Berkeley also experienced residential segregation during World War II. Having a higher proportion of African-

Americans in its population than any other Bay Area city during the war, Berkeley's black population concentrated itself in "South Berkeley." This area's boundaries ranged from Oakland on the south to Dwight Way on the north and from Grove Street on the east to San Pablo Avenue on the west. Ashby Avenue provided the chief thoroughfare for this region of South Berkeley.[22] Most of the homes in this section were comfortable single-family dwellings. Another area in West Berkeley paralleling San Pablo Avenue to Dwight Way and extending towards the industrial area adjacent to Aquatic Park did not fare as well as South Berkeley. Housing in this section of West Berkeley was substandard with overcrowded conditions.[23] During World War II, the relocation of Japanese families living in South Berkeley offered African-Americans the opportunity for housing in an area already heavily populated by black families; nevertheless, Berkeley's housing shortage continued. Many white families began to move away from racially mixed neighborhoods which further exacerbated the residential segregation of Berkeley.[24]

The Federal Public Housing Agency began to consider the construction of an emergency war housing project on vacant lots in northwest Berkeley between San Pablo Avenue and the Southern Pacific Railroad tracks. White residents of Berkeley, concerned by this prospect, lobbied the Berkeley City Council in August, 1943, to reject the proposed housing project. The Vice-President and General Manager of the Berkeley Chamber of Commerce, J. Delbert Sarber, expressed his concerns in a letter read at the Council meeting of August 20, 1943. It stated:

1. The Chamber of Commerce was against public housing.
2. The federal construction of emergency housing projects took land off the city tax rolls.
3. The Federal Housing Authority administration should make a thorough search for land elsewhere.
4. Private enterprise should be encouraged by the federal government to construct new housing.
5. There were sufficient building contractors in Berkeley to supply adequate housing for the wartime emergency.
6. Land could be found closer to the worker's place of employment.
7. The federal government had not proven the failure of Berkeley's private sector to provide adequate housing.

8. Berkeley's citizens did not desire change in their housing conditions.[25]

The Berkeley Manufacturers Association also expressed similar caveats to those of the Chamber of Commerce.

The Berkeley City Council received these protests at its August 20, 1943, meeting. Opponents of the housing project claimed that the proposed project would take land needed for the future industrial development of Berkeley. Councilman Redmond C. Staats chaired a committee of the Berkeley Council which prepared the draft of a letter sent to Washington, D.C., opposing the housing project.[26] The Federal Housing Authority replied that it had considered other available locations and needed the proposed site in order to carry out its responsibilities to a defense area. The Berkeley City Council adopted a resolution to take the issue to the Truman War Investigation Committee; yet, all its efforts failed when the Housing Authority built Cordonices Village in early 1944. The Council's reluctance to encourage federal housing project which would introduce of large numbers of African-American war workers into Berkeley did not go unchallenged. On January 19, 1944, W. Byron Rumford, a member of the Berkeley Inter-racial Committee, presented to the Berkeley Council a petition signed by 283 Berkeley residents seeking nondiscrimination in the selection of tenants for Cordonices Village. The Council responded that it was an issue for the federal government and that assignments had not yet been made. When the project opened in April, 1944, assignment of the least desirable units close to the Southern Pacific Railroad tracks went to African-Americans. It would not be until 1946 when continued demand of minority groups for housing ended *de facto* segregation in Cordonices Village through the introduction of a nondiscriminatory policy.[27]

By 1953 the federal government wanted to return the site of Cordonices Village to its private owners and to liquidate its investment in the Berkeley housing project. When eviction proceedings began in 1953, many residents refused to leave. One year later African-Americans comprised 88 percent of the inhabitants of Cordonices Village. Arthur Green acted as their spokesman and pointed to the large number of families who would have to be relocated. The Council appointed a committee to study the housing problem. Finally it resolved to relocate familes and return the vacated land to industrial development.[28] Exclusive white neighborhoods remained intact during this relocation. Groups such as the Claremont Improvement Club prevented African-Americans from occupying housing in white neighborhoods by bringing legal suits against them.[29]

African-American protests against discrimination in housing and employment opportunities escalated during World War II. Veteran organizers within the black community joined both local and nationwide campaigns to promote equal opportunity. C.L. Dellums not only worked closely with the city of Oakland to integrate Campbell Village, but he also helped A. Philip Randolph organize the March on Washington movement in early 1941. The idea for a March on Washington to highlight African-Americans' right to equal participation in defense work employment stemmed from A. Philip Randolph's recognition that the New Deal administration was not acting upon the demands for fair treatment. Randolph met with President Roosevelt; Undersecretary of War, Robert Patterson; the Secretary of the Navy, Frank Knox; Walter White of the NAACP; and T. Arnold Hill of the National Urban League on September 27, 1940, at the White House. Along with White and Hill, Randolph submitted a memorandum calling the immediate and complete integration of all defense preparations. Two weeks later on October 9, 1940, the President's secretary, Stephen Early, called a press conference to announce the War Department policy with regard to African-American participation in national defense. Early misrepresented the September 27 meeting with the President when he told the press:

> You will remember that . . . the President held a conference . . . with Walter White, and I think, two other Negro leaders. . . . As a result of that conference the War Department has drafted a statement of policy with regard to Negroes in national defense.

Early described the War Department's policy as precluding the integration of "colored and white enlisted personnel in the same regimental organizations."[30] Newspapers reported that the Roosevelt administration approved the segregation policy "after Roosevelt conferred with Walter White [and] two other Negroes."[31] "Shocked and amazed" at the impression Early gave the press regarding the September 27 White House meeting,

Randolph expected the White House to issue a public denial of
Early's statements. Early's subsequent personal behavior towards
African-Americans also concerned Randolph. Secretary Early kicked
a black New York City police officer in the groin when the officer,
assigned to protect President Roosevelt, refused Early permission
to cross a police line.[32] Although Walter White demanded that
Early be fired from the President's staff, Early remained as
Roosevelt's secretary. Instead, President Roosevelt wrote a letter to
White, Hill, and Randolph conceding that:

> . . .your position, as well as the attitude of both White House
> and the War Department, has been misunderstood. The plan . . .
> on which we are all agreed is that Negroes will be put into all
> branches of the service, combatant as well as supply.
> Arrangements are now being made to give without delay, training
> in aviation to Negroes. Negro reserve officers will be called to
> active service and given appropriate commands. Negroes will be
> given the same opportunity to qualify for officers' commissions as
> will be given to others.[33]

Although Randolph, White, and Hill quoted the President's letter
in public to clear their names, Randolph remained unconvinced that
traditional forms of protest—public statements, telegrams to
Washington, and conferences with White House officials—were
enough to achieve equal participation of African-Americans in
defense programs.

In December, 1940, Randolph proposed a new form of
protest—a march of 10,000 African-Americans down Pennsylvania
Avenue. Randolph and Milton Webster, First Vice-President of the
BSCP, began to introduce the idea of a march on Washington at
Brotherhood meetings throughout the South, and then black
newspapers across the nation began to report the idea as well. On
January 15, 1941, Randolph issued the following statement to the
press:

> . . . only power can effect the enforcement and adoption of
> a given policy, however meritorious it may be. The virtue and
> rightness of a cause are not alone the condition and cause of its
> acceptance. Power and pressure are at the foundation of the
> march of social justice and reform . . . power and pressure do not
> reside in the few, and intelligentsia, they lie in and flow from the

masses. Power does not even rest with the masses as such. Power is the active principle of only the organized masses, the masses united for a definite purpose. Hence, Negro America must bring its power and pressure to bear upon the agencies and representatives of the Federal Government to exact their rights in National Defense employment and the armed forces of the country. . . . I suggest that TEN THOUSAND Negroes march on Washington, D.C. . . . with the slogan: WE LOYAL NEGRO AMERICAN CITIZENS DEMAND THE RIGHT TO WORK AND FIGHT FOR OUR COUNTRY. . . . No propaganda could be whipped up and spread to the effect that Negroes seek to hamper defense. They want to do none of these things. On the contrary, we seek the right to play our part in advancing the cause of national defense and national unity. But certainly there can be no national unity where one tenth of the population are denied there basic rights as American citizens. . . . One thing is certain and that is if Negroes are going to get anything out of this national defense, which will cost the nation 30 or 40 billions of dollars that we Negroes must help pay in taxes as property owners and workers and consumers, WE MUST FIGHT FOR IT AND FIGHT FOR IT WITH GLOVES OFF.[34]

Randolph directed a March on Washington Committee (hereafter referred to as the MOWC) with regional committees set up in cities across the country with the support of the Brotherhood of Sleeping Car Porters' local divisions. C.L. Dellums headed the Oakland committee supporting a march on Washington. The proposed March on Washington excluded whites from participating in the protest. Dellums recalled telling his white friends throughout the nation that the march had to be a Negro one:

for the inspiration of Negroes yet unborn. We told them all we wanted was their moral support, to stand on the sidelines and cheer us on. We were unalterably opposed to segregation, but we also knew that Negroes needed an example of Negroes doing something for themselves. We didn't go for no separation stuff. That's South African.[35]

There has been considerable debate as to whether Randolph's claim to have 100,000 marchers converge on Pennsylvania Avenue represented a strategic bluff since many doubted that many African-Americans would respond to Randolph's call.

By March, 1941, Randolph issued an official call for a march on Washington to take place July 1, 1941. At the end of May he raised the number of marchers from 10,000 to 100,000. This alarmed the Roosevelt administration which tried to determine whether 100,000 African-Americans really planned to march on Washington. Jervis Anderson, in his biography of A. Philip Randolph, states that the local march committees could have turned out at least 10,000 marchers.[36] Whether there were 100,000 marchers or only 10,000 did not matter to the Roosevelt administration. The logistics of bringing groups of either size to Washington frightened the Roosevelt administration which remembered all too clearly the dire results of the Bonus Army March in 1932 upon the Hoover administration.

Randolph sent letters to Frances Perkins, Secretary of Labor; Sidney Hillman and William Knudsen at the Office of Production Management; Henry Stimson, Secretary of War; and Eleanor Roosevelt inviting them to address the marchers on July 1. Even Eleanor Roosevelt, a staunch supporter of African-American campaigns for equal rights, advised Randolph against holding a march on Washington saying that she felt "that if any incident occurs as a result of this, it may engender so much bitterness that it create in Congress even more solid opposition from certain groups than we have had in the past."[37] Stephen Early consulted with Wayne Coy at the Office for Emergency Management asking whether "it would not be possible, since this movement originates in New York, for you to appeal to Mayor La Guardia to exercise his persuasive powers to stop it."[38] A meeting with Mayor La Guardia, Eleanor Roosevelt, Walter White, and A. Philip Randolph was held in New York's City Hall on June 13, 1941. Concerned about where the black marchers would find food and shelter in Washington, D.C., where Jim Crow segregation flourished, Eleanor Roosevelt tried to dissuade Randolph from a march which might lead to violence. Randolph responded that:

> there would be no violence unless her husband ordered the police to crack black heads. I told her I was sorry, but the march would not be called off unless the President issued an executive order banning discrimination in the defense industry.[39]

Mayor La Guardia and Eleanor Roosevelt reported to the president that nothing would dissuade Randolph from the march unless the President spoke directly with his cabinet aides and Randolph. On June 18, 1941, the President met with Randoph; Walter White; Mayor La Guardia, William Knudsen and Sidney Hillman; Henry Stimson, Secretary of War; Robert Patterson, Under-secretary of War; Frank Knox, Secretary of the Navy; Anna Rosenberg of the Social Security Board; and Aubrey Williams of the National Youth Administration. President Roosevelt offered to call up the heads of defense plans and urge them to follow nondiscriminatory policies. When Randolph (with La Guardia's support) refused to call off the march on the strength of that offer, Roosevelt appointed a committee of five to draw up an executive order that would be acceptable to both himself and Randolph. Joseph L. Rauh, a lawyer in the Office for Emergency Management, submitted several draft proposals to Randolph by telephone until finally one was accepted. On June 25, 1941, President Roosevelt signed and issued Executive Order 8802 which stated "that there shall be no discrimination in the employment of workers in defense industries or government because of race, creed, color, or national origin" and that "it is the duty of employers and of labor organizations . . . to provide for the full and equitable participation of all workers in defense industries." Although the Executive Order did not address segregation in the armed forces, it did provide the foundation for fair employment practices without consideration of race. The Executive Order was enforced by a temporary Fair Employment Practices Committee appointed by the President to "receive and investigate complaints of discrimination" and to take "appropriate steps to redress grievances."[40] This committee served the President until 1946 and was charged with 1) upholding the principles of human rights and 2) maintaining an effective labor force for the defense industries engaged in the war effort. Alonzo Smith and Quintard Taylor make clear in their article, "Racial Discrimination in the Workplace," that it was the second charge "which was the more important factor in securing defense employment for African Americans."[41] The FEPC worked with the War Manpower Commission and the U.S. Employment Service to combat employment discrimination. Gunnar Myrdal closed his study of *An American Dilemma* by noting that:

> The March-on-Washington movement is interesting for several reasons. It is, on the one hand, something of a mass movement with the main backing from Negro workers, but has at the same time the backing of the established Negro organizations. Though a mass movement, it is disciplined and has not used racial emotionalism as an appeal. It demonstrates the strategy and tactics of orderly trade unionism. For the Negro cause it is prepared to use pressure even against the President. But it knows just how far it can go with the support that it has.[42]

Randolph used his position as President of the Brotherhood of Sleeping Car Porters to urge the American Federation of Labor to appoint a committee to investigate race bias in unions or employment opportunities. In Seattle, three months after the President announced Executive Order 8802, Randolph addressed the AFL convention and named unions whose racial policies were in violation of Executive Order 8802. Included among these were the Painters, Plasterers, Cement Workers, Metal Workers, Machinists, Boiler Makers, and Carpenters. All these unions were highly visible in defense industries. Trade unionists reacted predictably by referring to Randolph as a "professional Negro" and agitator.[43] Randolph repeatedly introduced antidiscrimination resolutions at the AFL conventions demanding that the Federation pursue a vigorous policy of organizing black workers and demand the cessation of excluding black members in unions affiliated with the AFL. The unions excluded African-Americans from membership by various methods including provisions within their constitutions and creation of auxiliary memberships with restricted privileges. Because of union closed shop agreements with industrial employers African-Americans could not be hired unless they were union members. This severely limited their ability to participate in shipyard work.

After the announcement of Executive Order 8802, A. Philip Randolph declared that the March on Washington Committee would become a permanent movement to serve as a watchdog over the order's enforcement and to campaign for a permanent Fair Employment Practices Commission. The local committees for the march created regional divisions with their own officers to continue pressure for fair employment practices.

The shipbuilding unions of the Bay Area barred African-Americans from participation in the skilled trades. C.L. Dellums recalled that:

> Some months after the president's committee was in operation there wasn't an identifiable Negro working in any shipyard [in Oakland, Sausalito, and San Francisco], and Kaiser alone had three or four in Richmond. I called [Milton] Webster and suggested they get Clarence Johnson and send him here to crack these shipyards. Webster called the committee's office in Washington and they went to work on it.[44]

Since Milton Webster, First Vice-President of the BSCP, had been appointed to the President's temporary committee on Fair Employment Practices, Dellums felt he would be able to send investigators to the Bay Area who could pressure the defense industries into compliance with Executive Order 8802. Webster succeeded in having Clarence Johnson sent from Washington, D.C. to the Bay Area. Johnson was a former Californian with a labor background in the Dining Car Cooks and Waiters Union on the Southern Pacific. He went to Washington to work for the Public Housing Administration and then found employment with the Fair Employment Practices Committee. In the fall of 1941 Johnson found that more than a third of the Bay Area's African-American labor force was unemployed or on relief. After Johnson arrived in the Bay Area he managed to place two African-American referrals in the Kaiser shipyards at Richmond.[45] This occurred shortly before the Japanese bombed Pearl Harbor.

The declaration of America's entry in World War II brought union policies of racial exclusion into conflict with the harsh realities of a nation at war. Two of the larger unions at Oakland's Moore Dry Dock absorbed African-American workers without delay. They were the C.I.O. Machinists' Union and the A.F.L. Laborer's Union which accepted unskilled shipyard maintenance workers.[46] Other unions responded slowly and grudgingly to inclusion of minority workers. The Boilermaker's Union issued work permits to a small number of African-Americans without consideration for future union membership.

During the summer of 1942 Frances Albrier completed double the number of training hours required for welding and applied for a job at the Kaiser shipyards in Richmond. Told that she could not be hired because the Boilermakers' Union at Kaiser had not established an auxiliary, Frances Albrier took the issue to the head of the Richmond yards and told him that she would go to the White House with charges that Kaiser's policy violated Executive Order 8802. Kaiser made special arrangements for her to work without union membership until Local A-36 of the Boilermakers, Iron Ship Builders and Helpers of America was established in February, 1943.[47] As the war continued, the union set up auxiliaries for minority workers who paid the same dues as members of the regular union. However, auxiliary members could not vote on union matters and could have their auxiliary status dissolved at any time by the discretion of the regular union local. Anyone who failed to keep in good standing with the auxiliary could lose his right to work under union protection and the employer would be required to fire the lapsed member. Between 1942 and 1944 over ten thousand African-Americans found themselves forced to join the auxiliaries or go without shipyard work.[48] The Teamsters' Union and the Steamfitters' Union in the Bay Area succeeded in maintaining exclusionary policies toward African-Americans by hiring large numbers of women who were accepted in lieu of black workers.[49]

The union auxiliary played an important role within the African-American community by lobbying for benefits aimed at helping not just workers but their entire family. Local A-36 succeeded in helping to place fifteen African-American women in Richmond's Recreational Department and raised funds for the purchase of a playground site in North Richmond. The shipyard workers in Richmond also organized the United Negro Labor Committee (UNLC) with help from white workers and Communist Party members. The UNLC campaigned for the national Boilermakers' Union to provide insurance benefits and extend the right to vote in union elections to members of union auxiliaries. In May, 1943, the UNLC and Local A-36 co-sponsored the celebration for the launching of the Liberty Ship, the *George Washington Carver*. A program of speakers and African-American dignitaries marked the *Carver's* launching from the Henry Kaiser shipyards in Richmond. Lena Horne came on stage as a sponsor along with C.L. Dellums as Vice-President of the Brotherhood of Sleeping Car Porters; Spencer Jourdan, Vice-President of the Brotherhood of Boilermakers; J.R. Hoskins, Vice-President of the United

Transportation Service Employees; and T.M. Anderson, Secretary-Treasurer of the Dining Car Cooks & Waiters Union.[50] The African-American's hope for equal participation and legitimacy in the East Bay found voice in the lauching celebration in Richmond and from the progress which wartime employment opportunities offered them. Katherine Archibald, who wrote about wartime shipyards in the Bay Area, concluded her study by saying that "the white worker in heavy industry and the skilled trades may still come to the table first and take the best seat; but now the Negro sits there, too."[51]

Examples of an improved environment for employment began to occur only months after the pronouncement of Executive Order 8802. The California State Employment Service conducted a survey in the fall of 1941 to register African-Americans according to their skills in an effort to eliminate the common practice of registering them only for menial work. In December, 1941, when an African-American rigger was refused employment by a riggers' union in Oakland because of race, the case was referred to the Oakland branch of the NAACP and then later to the Fair Employment Practices Committee. When the government chose to enforce fair employment practices, gains for minorities occurred. In 1942 even the military established an African-American training school for military police at Camp Ashby in Berkeley.

The major change which World War II brought to African-Americans living in California's East Bay derived from the assurance of fair employment practices which Executive Order 8802 offered them. For the first time since Reconstruction the federal government promised fair and nondiscriminatory treatment of minorities in federal employment and housing. Douglas Henry Daniels in his book, *Pioneer Urbanites: A Social and Cultural History of Black San Francisco*, recognized this change when he stated that World War II created the Bay Area's first black proletariat.[52] The experienced leadership of the African-American community quickly recognized this promise; and, pushed by newcomers anticipating the fulfillment of their California Dreams, these leaders used the Executive Order as a mandate to demand redress of grievances.

An example of this change in temperament can be identified in the litigation initiated by Joseph James, an African-American worker at Marinship. Although not located in California's East Bay, Marinship's court case, *James v. Marinship*, influenced African-

Americans throughout the Bay Area, especially those workers who commuted to Marinship from the East Bay. The case also involved the support and organizational contacts of Bay Area activists and local organizations.[53] Marinship became an "instant" shipyard created by the United States Maritime Commission at Sausalito in 1942. The Maritime Commission contracted with private companies to establish plants throughout the Bay Area. The huge Kaiser yards in Richmond was the first to be so commissioned. W.A. Bechtel Company of San Francisco won the contract for the Marinship yard at Sausalito, and, in June, 1942, laid its first keel there. Liberty ships, cargo vessels, and prefabricated tankers were among the vessels built at Marinship. Bechtel kept the yard in operation twenty-four hours a day, seven days a week. At first employing 15,000 workers, Marinship's yard increased until it had 22,000 workers there by 1943. By mid-1943, African-Americans comprised the largest minority group at Marinship.[54] The Marinship Corporation conducted a:

> massive training effort, taking paternalist pride in the 'indoctrination program which taught colored recruits who had never held a responsible job before, as well as those from the so-called underprivileged portions of the country, good work habits.'[55]

Some of the paternalism evident in the Corporation's training program spilled over to its housing efforts as well. Within three days the planning for a 200 acre site just north of the Marinship yard for worker housing was completed. The Bechtel Company used Maritime Commission funds to build Marin City housing a population of 5500 Marinship workers and their families. Attempting to make Marin City a model community, the Marin County Hosuing Authority and its Chief of Project Services, Miles C. Dempster, offered housing accommodations on a first-come, first-serve basis without regard to race.[56] Both African-Americans and whites served on the Marin City Council which was established to advise county agencies. It even published a weekly newspaper called the *Marin Citizen*. Not all Marinship workers found housing in Marin City. Restrictive covenants prohibited many minority workers from private housing accommodations in Marin County. Many African-American employees at Marinship found housing across the bay in the crowded Fillmore district of San Francisco. Inexpensive housing opened up in the Fillmore's "Japantown" after 1942 when its former Japanese-American residents were relocated to internment camps. By 1943 nearly 9,000 African-Americans crowded into housing that originally had been occupied by 5,000 Japanese-Americans.[57]

While African-American workers were actively recruited at Marinship, they labored under the restraints of the International Brotherhood of Boilermakers, Iron Shipbuilders and Helpers of America which represented about seventy percent of Bay Area shipyard workers.[58] During 1942 the Boilermakers' Union issued clearance certificates for African-Americans to work in the shipyards; however, by 1943, the union, pressured by large numbers of minority workers, established auxiliaries for its non-white workers. Although the NAACP filed a complaint regarding this policy with the National Labor Relations Board, the NLRB did not ban the practice of forming auxiliaries.

When Boilermakers Local 6 in San Francisco announced in August, 1943, that minority workers must join and pay dues to its auxiliary, A-41, in order to receive union work clearance, a committee of African-Americans living in San Francisco's Fillmore district organized as the San Francisco Committee Against Segregation and Discrimination. Joseph James, an African-American who came from the East Coast in 1939 to sing in Treasure Island's "Swing Mikado," became the committee's official spokesman. In addition to his singing career, committee work, and duties as president of the NAACP branch in San Francisco's, James became a leader among Marinship workers where he was a journeyman welder and member of Marinship's "flying squad" of welders used for special jobs. One week after Local 6 announced the formation of Auxiliary A-41, Marinship's company magazine, the *Marin-er*, took up the issue of race relations in the shipyard. A Negro Advisory Board headed by Joseph James helped prepare this special issue. James wrote the lead article, "Marinship Negroes Speak to Their Fellow Workers," and charged the paper's readers "to turn our hatred, instead of against each other, against the forces of fascism."[59] Condemning discrimination, other editorials claimed that victory in World War II would "prove for all time the dignity and rights of the individual man regardless of race, creed or color."[60] Ironically the racial tension, which the *Marin-er* tried to dispel during a summer when race riots erupted in Detroit and Los Angeles, began to surface at Marinship during the fall of 1943. Over 550 African-American workers in the shipyard refused to join the Boilermakers' Auxiliary A-41 and were warned on November 24, 1943, that if they did not pay their dues within twenty-four hours, they would be fired. The San Francisco Committee Against Segregation and Discrimination met that evening to discuss the union's ultimatum. Joseph James pointed out that the Committee's goal was not to destroy the union but to strengthen it by assuring Negroes the right to equal membership.[61] C.L. Dellums came from Oakland to help James establish that position and lend the group the benefit of his union experience in the BSCP. The participants unanimously agreed to continue boycotting Auxiliary A-41.

Acquiescing to the union demands, the management at Marinship refused permission to work on November 26 for approximately thirty African-Americans on the afternoon shift. Still more workers were refused to right to work on the graveyard shift. Early Saturday morning, November 27, 1943, hundreds of black men and women protested the lay-offs outside Gate 3 of Marinship's yard. The San Rafael *Daily Independent* described the protest which grew to over 800 people as "Marin's greatest labor demonstration and most critical situation to arise since the San Francisco 'general strike' in the summer of 1934."[62] Although Marin County Sheriff's deputies and Highway Patrolmen arrived at Gate 3 with nightsticks and tear gas, two African-American deputies from Marin City assured the Sheriff that they could keep order.[63] After meeting with company officials, Joseph James and three other Committee members, Preston Stallinger, Edward Anderson, and Eugene Small, addressed the crowd. James, Stallinger, and Anderson advised those who still had union clearance to return to their jobs while continuing to boycott Auxiliary A-41. Small counselled African-American workers "to stand pat and not return to work" until they received full union membership.[64] While the San Francisco *Examiner* estimated that 1500 workers were leaving their jobs in support of a strike, it is unlikely that the strike reached such large proportions as there were only 1100 African-Americans employed at Marinship.[65]

Failing to persuade workers to join the auxiliary under protest, Admiral Emory S. Land of the U.S. Maritime Commission asked

Marinship to suspend the lay-offs. California Attorney General Robert Kenny requested this when he pointed out that if ship production slowed down, "more American boys are going to die, both white American boys and black American boys."[66] The management, however, refused to suspend lay-offs citing its collective bargaining agreement which stated it was obligated to bar workers without union clearance. By Sunday, November 28, another 160 African-American workers were laid off, including Joseph James. On Monday morning, November 29, attorneys for the Committee Against Segregation and Discrimination filed a suit in the Federal District Court asking for reinstatement by Marinship and $115,000 in damages from the Boilermakers' union on behalf of Joseph James and seventeen other African-American workers.[67] A temporary restraining order suspending the lay-offs pending formal hearing of the suit was awarded by Judge Paul St. Sure. A second court order became necessary when Marinship halted lay-off procedures but refused to re-hire the 160 workers laid off on November 28 until they received union clearance. On December 3, 1943, the workers returned to work with union clearance slips.

On December 12, 1943, a formal hearing before Judge Michael Roche took place with Committee attorneys, George Anderson and Herbert Ressner, supported by Thurgood Marshall, Chief Counsel for the national NAACP, and Bartley Crum of the National Lawyers Guild. The union contended that the courts had no jurisdiction in this area and the case should be dismissed. Judge Roche referred the dismissal motion to a three-judge panel which announced on January 6, 1944, that "the plaintiff's action does not arise out of the federal constitution or any federal statutes" and therefore should be dismissed.[68] Although Boilermakers Local 6 announced it would withdraw union clearance for workers who had not paid auxiliary dues by January 14, 1944, attorneys for the Committee returned to court on that day filing suit using state rather than federal law. Marin Superior Judge Edward I. Butler of San Rafael issued a temporary order to avoid Marinship lay-offs.

Meanwhile President Roosevelt's Fair Employment Practices Commission investigated complaints against the Boilermaker's auxiliaries. Grievances came from African-American workers in the Pacific Northwest and southern California as well as California's East Bay industries. On December 14, 1943, the FEPC ordered the

Boilermakers' union to "eliminate all membership practices which discriminate against workers because of race or color."[69] Employers, including Bechtel and Kaiser, appealed the FEPC decision which meant new briefs would have to be filed. The appeal process took one year. FEPC chairman, Malcolm Ross, hoped to persuade the Boilermakers' union to change its policies when he addressed them at their International Convention in January, 1944, at Kansas City. On January 23, 1944, a mass meeting held in Oakland featured Joseph James, C.L. Dellums, and Committee attorney, George Anderson as speakers urging the abolition of auxiliaries. A white Boilermaker, Ray Stewart, also spoke at that meeting and said that "abolishing auxiliaries will benefit the union as much as the Negro." The East Bay Boilermakers Local 681 submitted a resolution to the International Convention requesting the union to allow full membership "without regard to race, color, creed, national origin or sex."[70] Submitted with the resolution were petitions carrying six thousand signatures from all Bay Area shipyards in support of Local 681's request.[71] Despite appeals against discrimination from African-American leaders as well as the AFL President William Green, the International Boilermakers convention ended with its leadership convinced that the auxiliaries' problems were the result of professional agitation among African-American trouble-makers. Boilermaker president, Charles MacGowan, claimed that the auxiliary problem was "not within the membership but with professional agitation attempting to make a cause where none exists."[72]

On February 17, 1944, Judge Edward Butler announced his decision in the case of *James v. Marinship* and ruled that the union's policy of "discriminating against and segregating Negroes into auxiliaries is contrary to public policy of the state of California."[73] Appealing the case to the California Supreme Court, the Boilermakers refused to accept African-Americans as full members but could not require auxiliary membership as a condition of employment at Marinship. Almost a year later, on January 2, 1945, the California Supreme Court handed down an unanimous decision supporting Judge Butler's contention that the practice of maintaining auxiliaries to union locals represented "racial discrimination" contrary to public state policy. The Court's decision stated that:

> A union may not maintain both a closed shop and a closed or partially closed membership as where its membership is closed to Negroes.
> Unions must be open to all who wish to join.
> When a union excludes Negroes from membership therein but insists that they must in order to work join a Negro auxiliary which does not give its members privileges . . . substantially equal to those given members of the parent union and which imposes unreasonable and discriminatory restrictions on Negroes who accept on terms of equality with other workers is the equivalent of a complete denial of union membership. Such discriminatory practices are contrary to the public policy of the United States and this State.
> Where a labor union has attained a monopoly of the labor supply through closed shop agreements, such unions, like a public service business, may not unreasonably discriminate against Negro workers for the sole reason that they are colored persons . . . .
> Use of economic pressure by a union that does not admit Negroes, to compel the discharge of Negro employees may be enjoined.[74]

The Boilermakers' union abolished its California auxiliaries only to create "separate but equal" all-black locals. This policy changed by 1948 when all Bay Area Boilermakers' unions in the Bay Area were racially integrated. Peacetime employment demands made their policies a mute issue as shipyard work declined drastically between 1945 and 1946. On May 16, 1946, even Marinship closed its yard while Joseph James returned to New York to pursue his singing career. The precedent for enforcement of fair employment practices had been set, and African-Americans still residing in the Bay Area took heart from it. As early as 1944, C.L. Dellums recalls proposals to "Make FEPC permanent for Jobs and Justice."[75]

While employment and housing concerns in the Bay Area monopolized the political efforts of most African-Americans during World War II, a more immediate area of concern was the treatment of black soldiers in the war effort. C.L. Dellums served two years on the East Bay Draft Board, No. 73—the only board in the country that employed African-Americans. Dellums said that out of eight employees, four were white and four were African-American. Although the Federal Bureau of Investigation kept a file on Dellums charging that he sent a dis-proportionate number of boys

Catalyst for Change 115

of Italian descent to the army and kept "[his] Negro friends' kids out," Dellums said the Board played no favorites:

> There was no favoritism on our board.... If you could justify deferment for your son, you got it. If you couldn't, you didn't. But the mere fact that he was of Italian descent and Mussolini in Italy was an enemy wasn't going to change us. The boys would never come to ask for deferments. It was their parents coming. We'd have boys come within a few hours after their parents had left and tell us, "I knew Momma was coming down here, but that's not me. I hope you didn't defer me." We'd say, "Don't worry, we didn't." But we never found any evidence that those youngsters themselves had any objections to going. It was the parents; and almost all of them, if they weren't immigrants themselves, were first generation. *Their* parents were still over there. So we had trouble; we had problems.[76]

The inclusion of African-Americans in the East Bay Draft Board marked a significant departure from the discriminatory treatment they received during World War I.

Despite the progress made by civilians in the Bay Area's Draft Board, the Armed Services remained segregated throughout the war with African-American personnel assigned to units commanded by white officers. During World War II, over one million African-Americans served in the U.S. Armed Forces, including 150,000 black seamen in the Navy. Although their numbers increased, African American soldiers continued to face discriminatory measures during World War II. The San Francisco Hospitality House and Dance Hall closed its doors to black servicemen. African American soldiers, excluded from recreation in San Francisco, traveled to Oakland where the East Bay Women's Welfare Club helped establish the only hospitality house for black soldiers on the West Coast in 1942. More than 300 black soldiers visited daily the De Fremery Park Hospitality House in Oakland. They came from several hundred miles to relax, play games, dance, sing, and converse at De Fremery. Chairing the De Fremery Hospitality Committee, Frances Albrier credited black women organizers for their industry, talent, and sympathetic hearts when it came to establishing De Fremery:

The house stands in the lovely old park, with its majestic trees and has become a rendezvous for boys of the armed services. Downstairs are reception and game rooms with a large hall for dancing and small kitchenette. There is a piano, a victrola and a few easy chairs, some books and magazines, lamps, tables anc drapes to make the place homelike and attractive. Miracles have been accomplished, yet much remains to be done. Many essentials are lacking, and with no fixed contributions from any source, it becomes a problem where to find them.[77]

By fall 1942, the Hospitality House became officially the De Fremery U.S.O. Club at 1651 Adeline Street in Oakland.

The irony involved in combating the racial policies of Adolph Hitler was not lost upon African-Americans fighting the war in racially segregated units. One of the first test cases for protesting racial policies in the U.S. Navy arose from a Bay Area tragedy at Port Chicago. Located on the present-day site of the Concord Naval Weapons Station, Port Chicago became one of the first naval installations to receive "general service" African-American personnel in 1942. In his book, *The Port Chicago Mutiny*, Robert L. Allen notes that "virtually all of the black seamen were relegated to mess duty or labor battalions."[78] During World War II Port Chicago became the principal West Coast port for loading munitions used in the Pacific theater.

Port Chicago's facilities included a ships' pier which extended into the Bay for 500 feet, a small barge pier, and twenty-seven barricaded sidings to accommodate 203 boxcars, nine storage buildings for inert materials, four barracks for enlisted personnel, a commissary, and a boiler house. Completed in November, 1942, Port Chicago loaded its first ship on December 8, 1942. The African-American enlisted personnel at Port Chicago were untrained for the work they performed: ammunition loading. Interviewing enlisted man, Joseph Small, Robert Allen writes that "Joe Small recounted that he rather casually 'picked up' the job of being a winch operator after watching other men operate the machines. He was never trained for the job."[79] The Longshoremen's union in June, 1944, warned the Navy that there would be a disaster in Port Chicago if the Navy continued to use untrained seamen to load ammunition. The Navy ignored the union's offer to send experienced longshoremen to train the Navy

Catalyst for Change 117

recruits. In addition to the lack of training at Port Chicago, the installation's commanding officer, Captain Nelson Goss, proved reluctant to receive minority recruits and held a low opinion of the working abilities.[80] Goss noted that "most of the men obtainable from these races do not compare favorably with those of the white race" and that many of the available white civilians were of "enemy alien descent" and therefore posed security risks to the naval installation.[81] The loading of ammunition at Port Chicago went on around the clock with divisions loading ships for two three-day stints of seven-hours per day, one day of "duty" when the division would clean up the grounds or unload dunnage, and one day of liberty. Workers at the installation called Port Chicago "a workhorse base" where "You'd go down in that ship and you build yourself all the way up—just packing until you find yourself way up on top."[82] In addition to the hard work, the white officers would pit their divisions against other officers' divisions and bet on which would be able to load the most tonnage.

On July 17, 1944, ninety-eight men of Division Three worked to load the *E.A. Bryan* so that by ten o'clock that evening it held approximately 4,600 tons of ammunition and high explosives, including naval shells, framentation cluster bombs, depth charges, rockets, incendiaries, fuses, detonators, guncotton, and smokeless powder.[83] Over one hundred men from Division Six were simultaneously working to prepare the *Quinalt Victory* for loading. At approximately 10:18 p.m. the disaster that the Longshoremen's Union predicted occurred when a massive explosion killed 320 seamen, 202 of them African-Americans. Another 390 military personnel and civilians were injured, including 233 African-American enlisted men. The copilot of an Army Air Force plane flying the radio range from Oakland to Sacramento at the time of the explosion described the scene from the air:

> We were flying on the right side of the radio range when this explosion occurred. It seemed to me that there was a huge ring of fire spread out to all sides, first covering approximately three miles—I would estimate it to be about three miles-m-and then it seemed to come straight up. We were cruising at nine thousand feet above sea level and there were pieces of metal that were white and orange in color, hot, that went quite a ways above us. They were quite large. I would say they were as big as a house of

a garage. They went up above our altitude. The entire explosion seemed to last about a minute. These pieces gradually disintegrated and fell to the ground in small pieces. The thing that struck me about it was that it was so spontaneous, seemed to happen all at once, didn't seem to be any small explosions except in the air. There were pieces that flew off and exploded on all sides. A good many stars and [it] looked like a fireworks display.[84]

The light of the explosion could be seen as far away as Alameda. Edward Coleman and his family were living next to the Todd Shipyard's repair section in July, 1944. As a new resident of Alameda, he remembered listening to the radio when Port Chicago's explosion occurred. Not certain of the time because:

it was like daylight twenty-four hours a day because the lights were on [in the shipyard]. When Port Chicago went off, it was startling. The whole sky went up. Everyone was out and a lot of people were really frightened. You couldn't see the fire, you just saw it lit up against the sky. I recall being a bit frightened because we just didn't know what was going on. The sirens were going off at the same time and people were scurrying around.[85]

When the *E.A. Bryan* was launched just five months prior to the Port Chicago explosion, her sponsor from Seattle, Mrs. Robert Hayes, turned to ask "How will I know what happens to her" after she broke a bottle over its bow.[86] The *E.A. Bryan* was destroyed in the 1944 Port Chicago explosion. All the men working aboard the *E.A. Bryan* were killed instantly, while the *Quinalt Victory* was split in two pieces which lifted into the air and returning as twisted chunks of metal. The pier was destroyed as well as sixteen boxcars and a diesel locomotive waiting for shipment. A survivor of the Port Chicago disaster remembered that "a boiling pillar of flame climbed two miles into the sky and a 30-foot-high-tidal wave swept across Suisun Bay."[87] Although the destruction of the *E.A. Bryan* and the *Quinalt Victory* would be the worst homefront disaster of World War II, little has been written about the explosion in the histories of the American homefront in World War II. Perhaps the mutiny trial which followed the explosion predisposed many to forget the incident as unworthy of historical notice.

On August 9 and 10, 1944, an assembly of the surviving seamen from Port Chicago met at Mare Island where the Navy ordered them to load ammunition ships. Fearing further unsafe loading practices, 328 seamen refused to return to work. Captain Nelson Goss then told his three division officers to issue individual work orders to each seaman whereupon seventy seamen agreed to return to work. However, not all the seamen received individual orders. On August 11, 1944, Admiral Carleton H. Wright addressed the remaining seamen who refused to load ammunition. After Wright's speech most of the men returned to work except for fifty seamen.[88] In a memorandum to Admiral Wright, dated August 13, 1944, Captain Goss gave his opinion of the problem stating that ever since African-Americans had been assigned to Port Chicago and Mare Island, there had been "agitators, ringleaders among these men." He thought that the seamen had been subjected to "outside propaganda and subversive influence." Goss characterized the Port Chicago seamen as having "a persistent disposition to question orders, to argue, and in effect to attempt to bargain." He referred in the memo to a "new characteristic" which he had "never observed before among Negroes"—sensitivity to discrimination.[89] Lacking a keen sense of perception, Captain Goss recommended that the fifty seamen refusing to work be charged with mutiny. Admiral Wright sent Captain Goss's recommendations to Washington, D.C., by August 13, 1944. For his part, Admiral Wright reported to Washington that he believed "a considerable portion of the men involved are of a low order of mentality...." Wright considered using black seamen to handle ammunition was a "logical use" of personnel, but conceded that "pains must be taken" to avoid the appearance of discrimination.[90] He also suggested the black seamen be given a rotation system whereby they occasionally received different assignments and duties. Also, Wright suggested that some white naval units be assigned the task of loading ammunition as well. James V. Forrestal, now Secretary of the Navy after replacing the deceased Frank Knox in the spring of 1944, approved Wright's recommendations and informed President Roosevelt that the measures would "avoid any semblance of discrimination against Negroes."[91]

The mutiny trial of the fifty black seamen from Port Chicago began on September 14, 1944, at Treasure Island Naval Base. The seven-man trial board had Retired Admiral Hugo S. Osterhaus as its president. Lt. Commander James F. Coakley became the chief prosecutor and trial judge advocate. He presented the testimony of officers who said they heard black seamen urging others not to load ammunition in order to show an organized effort of conspiracy to disobey orders. The five-man defense team, led by Lt. Gerald E. Veltmann, cross-examined prosecution witnesses who admitted that the defendants had been respectful and obedient in all orders except in their refusal to load ammunition. Most of the fifty seamen charged with mutiny testified that their actions stemmed from fear of unsafe loading conditions, not from a desire to challenge military authority. Most of the men said they were never given individual orders to load ammunition; and, if they had been given such orders, they would have obeyed them.

Although the defense team never identified discrimination as a justification for the actions of the accused seamen, African-Americans in the Bay Area believed discrimination existed in the Navy's treatment of the seamen at Port Chicago. Joseph James as President of the San Francisco branch of the NAACP said he was "well aware of the pattern of discrimination practiced in the navy and very much concerned about this trial. " Mrs. Irma Lewis of Oakland stated that "We mothers want to know why these loading crews are all Negroes." And J.C. Henderson, an Oakland attorney, said that "the discriminatory policy of the navy and the overall conditions to which the boys on trial have been subjected should be considered."[92] In late September, 1944, Joseph James asked for legal assistance from the national NAACP headquarters. On October 10, 1944, Thurgood Marshall, chief counsel for the NAACP, flew to San Francisco with special travel priority supplied by Navy Secretary Forrestal to observe the mutiny trial. Convinced the seamen were being unjustly prosecuted, Marshall said: "They have told me they were willing to go to jail to get a change of duty because of their terrific fear of explosives, but they had no idea that verbal expression of their fear constituted mutiny."[93] The mutiny trial lasted for thirty-three days; yet, within an hour and twenty minutes, the trial board ate their lunch and found all the defendants guilty, sentencing each seaman to fifteen years detention, reduction in rank to apprentice seaman, and a dishonorable discharge. Confirming the verdicts, Admiral Wright reduced on November 15, 1944, the sentences of forty men, due to their youth or lack of previous misconduct.[94] On April 3, 1945, Thurgood Marshall kept an appointment at the advocate general's office in Washington, D.C., where he delivered a prepared brief for the NAACP on behalf of the seamen. The advocate-general's office had already prepared a memorandum questioning several legal points made by the prosecution during the trial. On May 17, 1945, Admiral Wright was informed by Secretary Forrestal's office that the Secretary wished the court martial trial board would reconvene to reconsider the case without using hearsay evidence. Forrestal's office also accepted a definition of mutiny which would require a "deliberate purpose to usurp, subvert or override" authority. Meeting on June 12, 1944, the trial board met and "respectfully adhered" to its original verdict.[95] After the war concluded, the U.S. Navy officially announced that forty-seven of the accused sailors had been returned to active duty and would be given honorable discharges if they completed their service duties with good records. Two other defendants would be returned to active duty upon release from hospital treatment. Only one man was kept in detention because his conduct record did not warrant release.[96]

Changes in the Navy policies began quickly as the war ended. By June, 1945, all naval training facilities were integrated which would put an end to using untrained personnel in dangerous duties. In December, 1945, Secretary Forrestal ordered that "in the administration of naval personnel, no differentiation shall be made because of color."[97] He also appointed Lester Granger as his "special representative" to study race relations in the navy. An African-American graduate of Dartmouth, Granger had experience as executive secretary of the Urban League. He travelled some 50,000 miles visiting sixty-seven naval installations after his appointment from the Navy. He reported to Secretary Forrestal that he saw "very progressive changes" within the Navy on a month-to-month basis.[98]

Many African-Americans believed the changes were too sporadic and slow for real integration; however, the Navy had officially abandoned segregation. Walter Gordon summed up this change when he noted during the Mare Island mutiny trial that "any policy that brings about segregation based on race is bound to lead to points of conflict."[99] The African-American protest against segregation was centuries old at the end of World War II. Official denunciation of segregation through the federal enforcement of the Fair Employment Practices Act, the California Supreme Court's recognition of nondiscrimination as state policy in the case of *James v. Marinship*, and the U.S. Navy's new integration policies became the new harbinger of success for African-Americans during the Second World War. Heeding this herald of change, African-Americans in Oakland's East Bay would recognize the efficacy of mass protest during the next decades in order to achieve their dream for equality and legitimacy within the community.

NOTES

1. Albert S. Broussard presents the clearest picture of the African-American wartime migration in "Strange Territory, Familiar Leadership: The Impact of World War II on San Francisco's Black Community," *California History* 65 (March 1986): 18. Others who have acknowledged the strength of the pre-war leadership of the African-American community in Oakland's East Bay are Crouchett, Bunch and Winnacker, *Visions Toward Tomorrow*, 45.

2. Allan Spear, *Black Chicago: The Making of a Negro Ghetto, 1890-1920* (Chicago: University of Chicago Press, 1967). Spear compares San Francisco's population with that of Chicago during the nineteenth century.

3. Broussard, "Strange Territory, Familiar Leadership," 21-22.

4. "Explorations in Black Maritime History Exhibit," *Maritime Humanities Newsletter*, 2:1 (Spring 1983): 2, 5.

5. Edward Leon Coleman, interview by author, Tape recording, Eugene, Oregon, 11 May 1990.

6. *Ibid*. Segregation restrictions blurred somewhat as the trains moved westward. Edward Coleman saw African-American servicemen take seats on trains once they left St. Louis.

7. Henderson, *Tarea Hall Pittman*, 37.

8. Alonzo Smith and Quintard Taylor. "Racial Discrimination in the Workplace: A Study of Two West Coast Cities During the 1940s," *The Journal of Ethnic Studies* 8 (Spring 1980): 35-36.

9. Colbert goes on to say that "In the early days the in-migrant was considered as an evil that had to be endured because of the war. When these people began to purchase homes and to give all indications that they were here to stay the old-timers had to evaluate the influence their presence would have on the total picture." Robert E. Colbert. "Current Trends and Events [Section C]: The Attitude of Older Negro Residents Toward Recent Negro Migrants in the Pacific Northwest," *Journal of Negro Education* 15 (Fall 1945): 695, 701.

10. The term "pioneer urbanite" is borrowed from the title of Douglas Henry Daniels' book, *Pioneer Urbanites*. The term is especially appropriate for those pre-World War II residents who led African-Americans in the struggle for racial equality throughout the Bay Area. Daniels, *Pioneer Urbanites: A Social and Cultural History*

of Black San Francisco (Philadelphia: Temple University Press, 1980).

11. "Richmond Took a Beating: From Civic Chaos Came Ships for War and Some Hope for the Future," Fortune 31 (February 1945): 264.

12. U.S. Bureau of the Census, *Sixteenth Census of the United States: 1940, Housing*, 1 (Washington, D.C.: United States Government, 1940): 143.

13. *Oakland Tribune*, 21 January 1941, 1.

14. *Ibid.*

15. *Oakland Tribune*, 19 January 1944, 1.

16. *Ibid.*

17. *Ibid.* Cooper's testimony was repeatedly used by African-American agencies to encourage reform and better safety for shipyard workers living in Richmond.

18. *Oakland Tribune*, 21 January 1944, 1.

19. *Oakland Tribune*, 29 June 1948, 1.

20. Edward Everett France, "Some Aspects of the Migration of the Negro to the San Francisco Bay Area Since 1940" (Ph.D. diss., University of California, Berkeley, 1962), 33.

21. *Ibid.*, 43.

22. *Ibid.*, 47. In 1940 Berkeley's total population of 85,547 included 3,395 African-Americans (almost four percent of Berkeley's total population).

23. *Ibid.*, 47.

24. *Ibid.*, 48-49.

25. *Ibid.*, 49.

26. *Ibid.*, 49.

27. Helen Smith Alancraig, "Cordonices Village-A Study of Non-segregated Public Housing in the San Francisco Bay Area" (M.A. thesis, University of California, Berkeley, 1953).

28. France, "Some Aspects," 51.

29. *Ibid.*, 52.

30. Jervis Anderson, *A. Philip Randolph*, 244.

31. *Ibid.*

32. *Ibid.*, 245.

33. *Ibid.*, 246.

34. *Ibid.*, 248-249.

35. *Ibid.*, 254.

36. *Ibid.*, 257. In his book, *When Negroes March*, Herbert Garfinkel addresses the aspect of bluff when he said: "The March on Washington was either a real movement which swept up the Negro population of the country in a mammoth grass-roots activity or the Negro press throughout the country joined in putting over a fantastic hoax on the Administration." Herbert Garfinkel, *When Negroes March: The March on Washington Movement in the Organizational Politics for FEPC* (Glencoe, Illinois: The Free Press, 1959), 53.

37. Anderson, *A. Philip Randolph*, 252.
38. *Ibid.*
39. *Ibid.*, 255.
40. *Ibid.*, 259.
41. Smith and Taylor, "Racial Discrimination in the Workplace," 50, fn. 9.
42. Gunnar Myrdal, *An American Dilemma* (New York: Harper, 1944), 852.
43. Anderson, *A. Philip Randolph*, 292.
44. Henderson, *C.L. Dellums*, 97.
45. *Ibid.*, 98-99.
46. The C.I.O. supported integration of its workers, while the A.F.L. had a long history of opposing black workers within many of its unions.
47. Crouchett, Bunch and Winnacker, *Visions Toward Tomorrow*, 47.
48. *Ibid.*, 47.
49. Katherine Archibald in her study of Bay Area shipyards also points out that "admission of the Negro to a union, when finally it was gained, did not, of course, allow free access to the opportunities of the trade. On the job, the Negro was still subject to discriminatory practices. His were the less-favored, arduous tasks." Katherine Archibald, *Wartime Shipyard: A Study in Social Disunity* (Berkeley and Los Angeles: University of California Press, 1947), 81.
50. "Program of launching of *George Washington Carver* Liberty Ship," D, Carton 23, Folder: George Washington Carver launching. Cottrell L. Dellums Correspondence and Papers, Bancroft Library, University of California, Berkeley.
51. Archibald, *Wartime Shipyards*, 99.
52. Douglas Henry Daniels, *Pioneer Urbanites*, xiv-xv.

53. C.L. Dellums and the offices of Bay Area chapters of the NAACP were important contributors to the Marinship case.

54. African-Americans accounted for approximately ten percent of all Marinship employees in a largely multicultural workforce including Asian and Latin-Americans. Charles Wollenberg, "James vs. Marinship: Trouble on the New Black Frontier," *California History* 60 (Fall 1981): 264.

55. *Ibid.*

56. The *Christian Science Monitor* reported that Marin City proved that "white people and Negroes can live side by side-and get along." However a former Marin County Housing Authority official said that if the white majority were given power to eject blacks from the project, they would do so. *Ibid.*, 264-265.

57. San Francisco's health officials declared over half of the housing in the Fillmore district to be substandard. *Ibid.*, 266.

58. The agreement between the AFL Metal Trades Council and the Pacific Coast shipbuilders established a closed shop and specified that "all workers ... shall be required to present a clearance card from the appropriate union before being hired." *Ibid.*, 267.

59. *Ibid.*, 269.
60. *Ibid.*
61. *Ibid.*
62. *Ibid.*, 270.
63. *Ibid.*, 270.
64. *Ibid.*
65. *San Francisco Examiner*, 28 November, 1943, p. 1.
66. *Ibid.*
67. Wollenberg, "James v. Marinship," 271.
68. *Ibid.*
69. *Ibid.*, 272.
70. *Ibid.*
71. Charles Wollenberg in his article, "James vs. Marinship," points out that "of six thousand signatures gathered ..., about seventy-five percent came from white workers." *Ibid.*
72. *Ibid.*, 274.
73. *Ibid.*
74. France, "Some Aspect," 72; *James et al. v. Marinship Corporation*, 25, 721, 2nd California Reports (1944).

75. Cottrell L. Dellums Correspondence and Papers, Carton 23, Folder: March on Washington, Bancroft Library, University of California, Berkeley.

76. Henderson, *C.L. Dellums*, 84.

77. "Oakland Offers Negro Service Men Evening's Entertainment at De Fremery Hospitality House," *Oakland Tribune* (25 July 1942): 1.

78. Allen also notes that the mutiny by Port Chicago's African-American seamen was not an isolated incident within the Navy. Other mass protests and resistance occurred in October, 1943, when fifteen Seabees spoke against discrimination in the Navy and were dishonorably discharged; in December, 1945, when African-American sailors armed themselves to resist harassment by white marines on Guam; and, in March, 1945, when one thousand Seabees undertook a two-day hunger strike to protest Jim Crow practices with regard to promotion. Robert L. Allen, *The Port Chicago Mutiny: The Story of the Largest Mass Mutiny Trial in U.S. Naval History* (New York: Warner Books, Inc., 1989), 33, 34.

79. *Ibid.*, 42.

80. Captain Nelson Goss commanded the Mare Island naval depot in north San Pablo Bay of which Port Chicago was a sub-command.

81. Allen, *Port Chicago Mutiny*, 42.

82. *Ibid.*, 47.

83. John Stanley, "Search for Cause of Mysterious Explosion," *San Francisco Chronicle*, 3 June 1990, p. 47.

84. Allen, *Port Chicago*, 74.

85. Coleman, Interview with author, May 11, 1990.

86. "A Plate from Port Chicago," *Fore 'n' Aft* 44 (28 July 1944): 8.

87. In his review of Bob Anderson's documentary film, "The Mystery of Port Chicago," Stanley describes Anderson's meeting with Peter Vogel who believes that the Port Chicago blast was an atomic explosion. Vogel purchased a box of photographic supplies in 1980 at a rummage sale which contained a document apparently relating to an atomic explosion. Part of the document read: "The ball of fire mushroomed out at 18,000 feet in typical Port Chicago fashion." Vogel contacted Dr. Edward Teller who is reported to have told him: "I believe you have a classified document. I will never acknowledge having seen this or having discussed Port

Chicago with you." Vogel believes that the government chose Port Chicago as a blast site to test the bomb's effects. However, there is no evidence to support this theory. Stanley, "Search for Cause of Mysterious Explosion," *San Francisco Chronicle*, 3 June 1990, p. 48.

88. Initially only forty-four men refused to work; subsequently, another six seamen joined them.
89. Wollenberg, "Blacks vs. Navy Blue," 65-66.
90. *Ibid*.
91. *Ibid*.
92. *Ibid*., 69.
93. *Ibid*., 70.
94. Five men received eight years of detention, eleven men received ten years, and twenty-four men received twelve years. *Ibid*., 72.
95. *Ibid*., 72.
96. *Ibid*., 74.
97. *Ibid*., 73.
98. *Ibid*.
99. *Ibid*.

CHAPTER V

THE STRUGGLE FOR LEGITIMACY, 1945-1963

Between 1940 and 1960, the white population of California little more than doubled while the black population increased seven-fold from 124,306 to 883,861. Slightly more than ninety-four percent of the state's African-Americans settled in its urban areas, and, by 1960, comprised seventy percent of California's non-white population. Although wartime industries severely cut back their employees beginning in late 1944, the African-American population of California's East Bay did not decline. Elbert A. Daly, a newspaper publisher and migrant from Alabama in the 1920s, commented upon the influx of migrant workers who came to the Bay Area during World War II when he said, "If you were in prison and the doors were suddenly opened for you to go out, you wouldn't volunteer to go back in it, would you?"[1] African-Americans secured employment as laborers in wartime industries because those were the areas with the highest need for workers. When those industries declined during the postwar years, unemployed black workers began to look for new employment in skilled as well as unskilled labor. They also hoped to secure jobs in areas close to their homes. This meant that many industries and businesses which did not hire African-Americans before the war had to field numerous applications from skilled black workers after the war.

Before the war African-Americans had few employment opportunities in the municipal occupations of streetcar operators, bus drivers, and the police force. Unwilling to return to their pre-war status, African-Americans began a long struggle to secure better jobs and move into better housing after World War II.

Reflecting this change in conditons, Matt Crawford, a pre-war resident of Oakland and assistant director of the CIO Minorities Committee of California, commented upon the irony of postwar attempts to rectify discriminatory policies. Crawford said the struggle to integrate unions and secure better housing produced:

> the modern racist responses: segregated union locals and 'urban renewal' [for] whole sections of West Oakland where Blacks were concentrated were torn down. People were forced out into East Oakland.[2]

Those African-American families who could afford to do so bought homes in Berkeley where a postwar survey showed "eighty-seven out of ninety-one Black families in Berkeley owned homes—showing both their prosperity and the scarcity of rentals."[3]

Tensions built not only between white employers and black job seekers excluded from jobs because of their race, but also within the African-American community as well.

Cultural differences between the older residents of California's East Bay and the wartime newcomers created a sense of distinction and distrust among African-Americans. John Watkins, a native of Oakland, claimed he felt like a tourist in downtown Oakland after the war because he saw so many newcomers who dressed, talked, and acted differently from the older residents. Going to a restaurant, Watkins and his friend asked for a second helping of potatoes. When the bill came, Watkins was charged ten cents more than his friend because he had asked for "potatoes," while his friend asked for "tatoes."[4] Even in speech patterns, the newcomers resented what they perceived as an attitude of pretense and superiority from the older residents. These differences in attitude were noticed by Bay Area residents even before the end of the war. In 1944, a race riot broke out on an Oakland train carrying over two thousand white and black servicemen and civilians. The *Oakland Observer* claimed the riot stemmed from:

> a semi-mining camp civilization and . . . a new race problem, brought about by the influx of what might be called socially-liberated or uninhibited Negroes who are not bound by the old and peaceful understanding between the Negro and the white in Oakland.[5]

The well-established African-American organizations of the Bay Area, such as the NAACP and the Urban Leagues of Oakland and

Richmond, helped to ameliorate the suspicions of both older residents and newcomers to the area by highlighting the need to present an united front to combat discriminatory policies in employment and housing. Usually a representative from NAACP or the Urban League would encourage job seekers to apply for employment in businesses suspected of discriminatory hiring practices; then the representative would document the employer's response to the applicant. If unfair practices appeared to be used against the applicant, the NAACP or Urban League would encourage boycotts against the business. Pickets bearing the words "Don't Buy Where You Can't Earn" often were placed outside of establishments with varying success. In those areas where businesses depended upon a large number of African-American customers, the boycotts often succeeded in opening up a position for black workers. If the establishment did not depend upon African-American customers, the boycotts did not have much success. The boycotts helped to publicize discrimination against African-Americans and raise the community's awareness. The National Maritime Union (NMU) aided this cause by running articles emphasizing the need for integration. In its publication, *Pork Chops*, the NMU carried an article entitled "Discrimination Costs You Money." It said:

> Racial discrimination is one of the main tools used by employers to keep down wages, to keep their workers split and weak. When the rank and file seamen broke away from the phony, corrupt leadership of the SIU in 1937, one of the big lessons they had learned was that in their new union, the NMU, there should be no discrimination.
>
> The NMU has pioneered in the fight against discrimination. It has shown the country that white and Negro seamen can live together in harmony. NMU members have tried it and it works.
>
> The real backers of discrimination are bosses: interested in profits. By stirring up racial strife and distrust they hope to divide the workers. Then they can play white against Negro, American against Filipino, gentile against Jew, English-speaking against Spanish-speaking, and easily weaken each group.

This is happening in certain seamen's unions today. The SIU jim-crows Negroes. Harry Lundeberg, president of the SIU and secretary-treasurer of the SUP, kicked out all Filipinos from the SUP in 1934.

That's why the SIU is and always will be weak; in fact, the tool of the owners.

That's why the NMU is strong. That's why an NMU member tries to overcome his own prejudices. He knows the fellow who uses terms like "nigger," "ringtail," "spig," is being a sucker for the bosses. He knows unity means pork chops.[6]

Numerous issues of the *People's World*, a Communist publication, carried articles and photographs showing African-Americans seeking fair employment. On June 12, 1948, the *People's World* showed both black and white women of a NMU Joint Auxiliary Strike Committee meeting to make plans for a Mobile Canteen for striking pickets and a child-care program for working mothers.[7] Another article concerning the Maritime Cooks and Stewards Union said: "Rotary hiring means equality of opportunity for work to all members regardless of race."[8]

A decade earlier, African-Americans had little recourse when denied employment on account of race. William Byron Rumford failed the state oral examination for the position of food and drug investigator for the California State Board of Pharmacy because the examiners refused to ask relevant questions. The answer which seemed to displease the examiners the most came in response to their question as to whether Rumford thought Joe Louis was a good fighter. Rumford said he believed Louis to be an excellent prize fighter and doing a good job in his profession. After this comment, Rumford quickly found himself dismissed by the examiners.[9]

Both the NAACP and the Urban Leagues helped to break down these discriminatory policies by challenging the policies of a major streetcar employer in the Bay Area. The Key Route Transit System with its headquarters in Oakland refused to hire African-Americans despite the fact that during the war it lost many white workers to the higher paying wartime industries. Mrs. Lucie McCurry gave a statement to the NAACP on February 10, 1945, concerning her application for employment at the Key System's offices. She was told "this union local did not take in Negro Americans."[10] James Williams was told on November 22, 1944, that he was turned down as a platform man because of race.[11] The Key System maintained a requirement that motormen and conductors on its streetcars must pass an exam which African-American applicants failed to pass due to a time limit. C.L. Dellums claimed "that they didn't force whites to comply with the time limit but did force Negroes."[12] A stop watch was used to time African-Americans taking the exam. By 1945, a copy of the Key System's exam was obtained by a NAACP worker through the exam's publisher in Philadelphia. The NAACP led study sessions where the exam questions were drilled into prospective black applicants. The Key System allowed applicants twenty minutes to take the exam. After the NAACP study sessions, twelve black applicants successfully passed the exam; whereupon, they were sent to the Key System's company doctor who found them all physically unfit. According to Dellums, the applicants all looked like Joe Lewis. The NAACP intervened and sent the rejected applicants to other doctors who found them "fit as a fiddle."[13] Dellums, heading the Oakland chapter of the NAACP at the time, sent the applicants back to the Key System's company doctor who found the applicants to be healthy upon a second examination.

Next the NAACP found that the Key System maintained a closed shop agreement with the local carmen's union. Knowing that Oakland's local had affiliated with the A.F.L.'s Amalgamated Streetcar union, Dellums asked A. Philip Randolph to encourage the head of the international union to place pressure upon the Oakland local to observe the antidiscrimination clause within the Amalgamated Streetcar Union's constitution. Even pressure from the international body failed to sway the Key System from its discriminatory policy.

Randolph then asked the President's Commission on Fair Employment Practices to hold public hearings on the Key System in Oakland. An officer of the commission came to Oakland in and held hearings in the council chambers of the Oakland Board of Supervisors. In addition, Harry L. Kingman, head of the wartime FEPC, obtained information as to how the closed shop agreement came about. Dellums recalled that:

it was brought out during these public hearings that the committee workers here, through Harry Kingman, were prepared to produce proof that the Key System themselves called the union in and made a deal with them to give them a closed shop agreement if they would take the responsibility of keeping Negroes off the streetcars.[14]

The hearings lasted for three days and resulted in a public statement by the Key System that it would comply with any and all directives issued by the FEPC. Unfortunately no directives were issued because Congress killed the FEPC before directives could be drafted.

The San Francisco Urban League continued the assault upon the Key System initiated by the NAACP when it placed Kenneth Smith, its representative, in Oakland to negotiate with the streetcar management. When the Key System asked the Public Utilities Commission in 1951 for a reduction of service extended to certain areas due to a manpower shortage caused by the Korean War, both Smith and the NAACP asked the commission to deny the request. The Key System could not continue to refuse employment to qualified African-American applicants after the Commission heard evidence given by Smith and the NAACP, and by the end of 1951 the Key Route Transit System employed its first black bus driver.

The struggle to obtain fair access to employment in the Bay Area escalated during the postwar years throughout Oakland's municipal services, including its Fire and Police Departments. The NAACP sought to integrate Oakland's Fire Department beyond its policy of accepting African-Americans as firemen for only one station—Engine House 22 in north Oakland on Magnolia and 34th Streets. This limited the black firemen's chances for advancement. After working on this situation for nearly twenty years, the NAACP won a public statement of policy from Oakland's Fire Department in 1949 stating that nondiscrimination in assignments would be followed.[15]

In 1946, the State of California published the *Police Training Bulletin*, a training manual designed to establish better race relations between police officers and their communities. The bulletin developed from a course of training given in the Police Department of Richmond, California. At the invitation of the city of Richmond, Mr. Davis McEntire of the American Council on Race Relations prepared a curriculum and conducted courses in collaboration with the State Attorney General's office for police training.[16]

Racial tensions were high at this time. Tarea Pittman described conditions extended to African-American prisoners in Bay Area jails after the war as "completely segregated." She recalled that there were no sanitary facilities or adequate supervision of black prisoners in 1947. A prisoner could not come up for arraignment until Monday morning if arrested after Friday night in Oakland.[17] According to C.L. Dellums, police officers were rotated out of West Oakland if they did not write up enough traffic violations on African-Americans there. Dellums claims the Oakland police had a quota system. In addition, theft of money from Negroes arrested by the Oakland police was a common occurrence.[18] As President of the Alameda County Branch NAACP in 1950, Dellums opened hearings on police brutality in Oakland. He turned the hearings over to Robert B. Powers from the State Attorney General's office. The hearings were a joint effort involving the offices of Dellums, and State Assemblymen, Augustus Hawkins from Los Angeles and, after 1948, W. Byron Rumford, the first African-American from northern California to be elected to the Legislature.

One statement brought out at the hearings came from the case of Albert L. Hines, an unemployed African-American cannery worker. He had been shot to death by Spencer O. Amundsen, an Oakland Police officer, on Easter Sunday morning at daybreak. Hines had walked from his room to that of his friends within the same rooming house when he was shot by the police officer. Testimony given stated that Hines had his arms in the air when he was shot. The Coroner's jury rendered a verdict of "justifiable homicide" although the evidence presented little grounds for believing Hines was doing anything illegal. When rooming house friends asked why he shot Hines, Amundsen responded: "Because he was prowling outside your window." Yet for Hines to reach the main door of the rooming house from his own room it was necessary to pass the windows of his friends' room. The Oakland NAACP claimed that this was "only the worst in a long series of cases of Oakland Police brutality and terrorism."[19]

The police brutality hearings convinced many black leaders that efforts to strengthen political activism in the Oakland community were needed. As concern for a strong political voice grew, many individuals began to rally towards the Fair Employment Practices bill suggested by Augustus Hawkins, African-American assemblyman from Los Angeles. Hawkins recognized the need for a statewide Fair Employment Practices Commission (FEPC) even before World War II ended, and he introduced the first Fair Employment Practices bill to the state legislature in 1945. The national March on Washington Committee headed by A. Philip Randolph conceived the concept of choosing five states which would introduce statewide legislation for FEPC bills that year.

The following year, Randolph supported an initiative petition to create a statewide FEPC. This initiative reached the ballot in November, 1946. Because Earl Warren had cross-filed on both the Democratic and Republican gubernatorial tickets and won both party nominations in the primary election in June, 1946, he did not have to take a position on the Fair Employment Practices Act in November. Although C.L. Dellums opposed the initiative in 1946 because he believed "that nobody has a right to vote on whether or not I have a right to live, to work, and to make a living," he believed that the initiative failed because it did not have Warren's support.[20] By the following year, Dellums joined Hawkins in supporting legislative adoption of a Fair Employment Practices Commission in California. Assemblyman Hawkins continued to propose an FEP act yearly in the legislature until 1951 when he began alternating leading the FEP campaign with William Byron Rumford. Action on FEP legislation often would be blocked by a tie vote in the Rules Committee as occurred in 1950.

The 1948 election of William Byron Rumford to the California Legislature proved instrumental in the struggle to obtain a Fair Employment Practices Commission for California. Having been appointed by Governor Warren during World War II to the Berkeley Emergency Housing Commission which mediated between landlords and minority defense workers in need of housing, Rumford quickly became a representative for nondiscrimination in housing.

In 1944, Governor Warren appointed Rumford to the Berkeley and regional rent control boards and later to the California Housing Commission. Rumford's work captured the attention of the African-American community where both Democrats and Republicans sought to encourage him to run for political office. When Edward J. Carey refused to seek reelection for the Seventeenth Assembly District seat, a public meeting was held at the Beebe Memorial

African Methodist Episcopal Temple in Oakland in March, 1948, to discuss the selection of a black candidate for the Democratic primary held in June of that year. Although Rumford went to the March meeting to support another candidate, he found himself nominated for the position. He was accepted as a candidate by Democratic Party regulars and CIO union leaders present at the meeting. Rumford won the Democratic primary in June and faced Edgar S. Hurley, a conservative Republican with AFL support, in the November election.

Hurley ran his campaign on a platform based upon anti-unionism and open antipathy towards racial minorities in the state. Rumford capitalized upon Hurley's past performance as an Assemblyman when he was in the Legislature during the 1920s. Pointing out that Hurley voted against bills to improve conditions for labor and the elderly, Rumford also brought up Hurley's sponsorship of a poll-tax bill to disenfranchise non-whites. His campaign proved successful as Rumford won by a wide margin over Hurley.[21] The night before Rumford's installation as a new Assemblyman in the Legislature he was refused a room at the William Land Hotel across the street from the Capitol because of his race. Although the hotel manager finally showed Rumford to a room, this incident confirmed the new Assemblyman's desire to push through civil rights laws for California.

After Governor Warren addressed the joint legislative session on January 3, 1949, he called Rumford to his office where:

> he expressed the wish that I push through some civil rights bills, and promised that if they were passed he would surely sign them into law. He specifically urged me to press for legislation to abolish racial discrimination in the state National Guard.[22]

Rumford quickly became a spokesperson in the Assembly for minority rights. During his first month in office, he proposed two civil rights measures. He also introduced a rider to Richard H. McCollister's bill petitioning the federal government to allow National Guard units to come under state jurisdiction. Rumford's rider added a ban on racial discrimination in the National Guard when it came under state jurisdiction.

Because Assemblyman McCollister saw the rider as an obstacle to passage of his bill, he opposed it; however, the hearing committee passed it with few other Democratic rejections. The Assembly, controlled in 1949 by the Democratic Party, passed the bill and rider by a vote of 47 to 17. When the bill and rider reached the Assembly they were amended so much that Rumford decided the amended bill might actually strengthen discrimination in the National Guard. His concern that the Senate amendments took away an enforcement clause against discrimination led Rumford to oppose the bill as it appeared in the Senate. Finally the Senate Committee on Military and Veterans Affairs rejected both the bill and its rider.

Mindful of Governor Warren's support for an integrated National Guard, Rumford introduced his own bill (AB 807) prohibiting California National Guard units from segregation and racial or religious discrimination. California's legislation to integrate its National Guard units occurred fifteen years before the Gesell Committee reported to President Johnson in 1964 that one segment of the armed forces, the National Guard, had not been fully integrated.[23] San Francisco and Los Angeles maintained segregated units for African-American guardsmen throughout the state in 1949. Although black guardsmen might train with other community units, they remained as detached servicemen from either the San Francisco or Los Angeles units. Rumford's inclusion of an anti-discrimination clause in his National Guard bill prevented minority guardsmen from being reassigned to integrated units at a lesser rank than they held while in the segregated units at San Francisco and Los Angeles.[24] While Attorney General Fred N. Howser opposed the bill fearing that federal money might be withheld if it passed, Rumford encouraged liberal white support for his bill. It went through the Assembly's Committee on Military and Veteran Affairs and received the approval of the full Assembly. However, the bill bogged down in the Senate's Committee on Military and Veterans Affairs where hearings on the bill were delayed and then held at night when it was difficult to obtain a quorum. Rumford appealed to the committee members to attend the meetings so that the bill would not die in the committee. On June 27, 1949, the bill succeeded in getting enough committee votes to push it on to the Senate floor where it was passed on June 30, 1949. Governor Warren signed the bill into law on July 18, 1949.

The second bill which Rumford introduced to the Assembly in January 1949 called for insurance companies in the state to end

Struggle for Legitimacy

their practice of refusing to issue policies for automobile coverage to African-Americans and other minority groups throughout the state. Arguing that California required car owners to carry an insurance policy for public liability, Rumford claimed it was unconstitutional to refuse insurance due to race, color, or creed. He claimed that insurance companies that did grant coverage to African-Americans raised the premium by as much as fifteen percent. Passing both houses of the legislature, Warren commented upon signing Rumford's second bill (AB-32) that "It's about time we end these discriminatory practices."[25]

Aware that employment practices in California often worked against minority hires, Rumford co-authored a law to prohibit public school districts from using photographs and letters of reference as part of the process for hiring teachers. Along with Augustus Hawkins, Rumford recognized the need for a permanent Fair Employment Commission which would be forceful enough to impose financial penalties (up to $500) and jail sentences on employer groups discriminating on the basis of race, color, or creed.

The NAACP began to actively support the proposals made by Rumford and Hawkins for a statewide FEPC in the early 1950s. By the end of World War II, the NAACP had created its West Coast Region #1 consisting of seven states. By 1951, the West Coast Region of the NAACP led the mobilization for support of an fair employment practices act in Sacramento with Tarea Pittman as the group's organizer. Dellums wrote to Governor Warren requesting a conference on the Fair Employment Practices bill, but the governor refused. Instead, Dellums held a conference at a church in Sacramento near the Capitol and invited all eighty members of the California Assembly and the forty members of the California Senate to come to the meeting and sit on the platform. Only three assemblymen came: Augustus Hawkins, W. Byron Rumford, and Vernon Kilpatrick, a white assemblyman from Los Angeles who supported the FEP bill. Despite the small show of legislative support for the FEP bill in 1951, mobilizations led by the NAACP and the California Fair Employment Practices Committee continued to grow. They were held in odd-numbered years and grew from 100 supporters in 1951 to a crowd of over 1000 people in 1959.

In his oral history, C.L. Dellums explained the power which the FEP law had for change in society. He said:

> The FEPC law changed the people. It is a form of education. The best form of education is legislation. Organization, education and agitation helps. And of course force. By law or judicial decree. Then people actually see that their prejudices, which are fears, were largely imaginary and everything is really better.[26]

This belief helps to explain the conviction held by the African-American community in California's East Bay that the struggle for legitimacy through political and economic organization could succeed.

In late 1952, after another failure to promote statewide fair employment legislation, C.L. Dellums met with labor and civil rights activists at the San Francisco headquarters of Earl Rabb for the purpose of building a statewide organization to support a Fair Employment Practices act. Representatives from the AFL and the CIO came to the meeting which resulted in proposals for a statewide conference to be held in Fresno to launch an official organization. Dellums was elected Chairman for the Fresno conference with C.J. Haggerty from the California Labor Federation; John Despol of the CIO; Nat Colley; Ed Roybal, city councilman for Los Angeles; and Msgr. O'Dwyer of Southern California. The group became known as the California Fair Employment Practices Committee and by 1953 actively campaigned for FEP legislation. During that year, Augustus Hawkins worked within the California Assembly to attach the essentials of his FEP act to a bill that was considered a "must" bill in the Senate. The Assembly accepted the bill with the amendments made by Hawkins; however, the Senate rejected it with all Senate Republicans voting against it. Because the senators defeated the bill by a roll call vote, the California FEP Committee knew for the first time the names of legislators upon whom they could rely. This would prove instrumental in defeating senators who campaigned for reelection after that year. C.L. Dellums recalled the successful efforts made by volunteers to campaign against Senator F. Presley Abshire (Sonoma County) after he voted against the Fair Employment Practices bill.[27]

After the establishment of the California FEP Committee, the number of lobbyists for an FEP bill greatly increased. Most of the lobbyists represented civil rights organizations, church groups, and labor organizations. A survey taken in Richmond during 1954 showed that "seventy percent of the area's employers discriminate in employment."[28] The measure introduced by Assemblyman Rumford for an enforceable FEP law in 1955 stipulated that a provision for conciliation and educational services be made to implement the fair employment practices policy; that fines (up to $500) and sentences (up to six months in jail) be levied; and that a full-time five person commission be appointed by the Governor to administer the program. The *Oakland Tribune* reported that opposition to the Fair Employment Practices bill remained strong in 1955. It pointed out that the California State Chamber of Commerce, the Los Angeles Merchants and Manufacturers Association, the Associated Farmers, and the San Francisco and Los Angeles Chambers of Commerce went on record as opponents of the Rumford bill. The *Tribune* quoted L.C. Venderlip, legislative representative of the State Chamber of Commerce, as declaring that "Passage of an FEP Act in California would undoubtedly be a deterrent to future industrial development."[29] The San Francisco Chamber of Commerce maintained that the objective of fair employment practices should be achieved through education rather than compulsion. Randolph Van Ostrand, a representative of the Merchants and Manufacturers Association, said the:

> need for FEP is grossly exaggerated while minorities—Negroes, Mexicans, Orientals—are of doubtful value as employees since they have a high percentage of 'absenteeism' from the job.[30]

These comments reflect a sampling of employer opposition to the FEP bill in 1955, and indicates the strength of racial discrimination throughout the state.

According to Dellums, labor organizations and NAACP branches supplied over ninety percent of the money used to finance the California FEP Committee's efforts.[31] By 1958, the efforts of these groups resulted in a reconstruction of the Senate Labor Committee which meant a favorable recommendation for the FEP bill the following year. The lobbyists went to senators they believed were in favor of the FEP bill and asked them to make the Senate Labor Committee their first choice when they returned to the Assembly for a new term. Believing that the lobbyists would not be able to find out their committee preferences, many senators told the lobbyists that they would choose the Labor Committee first and then did not follow through.³² Dellums learned that John Holmdahl, representing Oakland in the Senate at that time, agreed to list the Labor Committee first but, in actuality, listed it as his third choice.

Before the FEP bill could reach the Labor Committee, it had to be assigned to that committee. Dellums spoke to Hugh Burns, a Democrat from Fresno in the senate, and asked that he not move the FEP bill in 1959 from the Labor Committee because Dellums did not want it to go to Luther Gibson's committee on Government Economy and Efficiency. Gibson's committee was known as the senate graveyard for most bills.

Although Hugh Burns did not comply with Dellums's request, George Miller, a senator from Martinez, managed to have the bill sent to the Labor Committee after all.³³

While the Labor Committee deliberated on the FEP bill, an administrative assistant from Gibson's Committee on Government Economy and Efficiency came to the Labor Committee suggesting thirty-one amendments to the bill. Those amendments were rejected but the Labor Committee accepted amendments presented by Senator Gene McAteer of San Francisco. Senator McAteer requested changes that Governor Warren suggested to him. The most important of these amendments changed the bill's request for a full-time commission to a part-time one.³⁴ Tarea Pittman, the NAACP's full-time lobbyist in Sacramento for the FEP bill after 1953, said that although she had many conferences concerning the FEP bill with legislators and government officials as a legislative advocate, Governor Warren never conferred with her. Pittman's experience with Warren's successor, Edmund (Pat) G. Brown, was far different. Brown:

> felt FEPC was morally right and that discrimination based on race or sex or national origin was immoral and this kind of thing. But we never had any conference like that with Warren.³⁵

When Brown campaigned for governor, he said that if were elected he would not only take the leadership in fighting to get FEPC, he would sign it into law. Under Governor Brown, the FEPC went became law and went into effect on September 18, 1959. Since employer groups and the State Chamber of Commerce fought a statewide Fair Employment Practices Commission for over fourteen years, Governor Brown recognized the need to choose a chairperson for the FEPC who would be respected by the business community. As a result, he chose John Anson Ford, liberal chairman of the Los Angeles Board of Supervisors, to head California's new part-time commission. The responsibilities of the commission's chairperson included assigning cases to the commissioners, presiding over FEPC meetings, and acting as official spokesperson for the commission. Brown's appointments to the FEPC helped to allay fears held by the business community about the new commission and ultimately led to the commission's acceptance by employers as a welcome advisor in labor relations.

Although the creation of the Fair Employment Practices Commission represented the most crucial legislation passed during 1959, two other civil rights bills passed the legislature that year which helped to end the blatant discrimination which African-Americans faced in California. Jesse Unruh's amendment to Section 51 of the California Civil Rights Code proposed that business establishments could not deny service to persons on account of race. Stating that:

> all persons within the jurisdiction of the State are free and equal, and entitled to the full and equal accomodation, advantages, facilities, and privileges or services in all business establishments of any kind whatsoever.

Unruh's bill echoed the political demands being made by Civil Rights activists in the South.

Another bill, AB 801, introduced by Augustus Hawkins in 1959 prohibited racial discrimination in housing sales financed by mortgages insured or guaranteed by the Federal Housing Administration or the Veterans Administration. Although this became law in 1959, it did not provide a strong deterrent as it punished violators with only a minor penalty. The bill's strength rested in its establishment of a Commission on Discrimination in Housing which provided a necessary forum for housing problems throughout the state.

The history of fair housing proposals for California's East Bay represented a long struggle by African-Americans against restrictive covenants, segregated federal housing projects, and sub-standard living conditions. As early as the late 1940s, the California Council of Negro Women concerned itself with raising the standards of black homes throughout California. The Council recognized that black women worked outside the home in greater proportion to their numbers in the general population and needed legislation for childcare centers, nursery schools, and safer neighborhoods for their children while their mothers were at work.[36] The Council succeeded in mobilizing African-American women throughout California for political action on housing and childcare issues. In 1949 the Oakland City Council designated West Oakland as a "blighted" area and targeted it for massive demolition. By this time African-Americans comprised over eighty-five percent of West Oakland's population. When the city of Oakland constructed its first low-income housing project, Campbell Village, in 1940, it set a precedent for construction of low-income housing which would be followed for several decades. Oakland purchased existing buildings at a low price and then demolished these dwellings to make way for low-income housing. As a result, many home owners opposed low-income housing projects fearing that their homes would not be sold at high market value. This certainly increased the tension and animosity which already existed between the older pioneer residents (many of whom were home owners in West Oakland) and those migrants arriving in California's East Bay during and after World War II. The belief that many of the demolished structures could have easily been repaired also angered the tenants who found themselves dislocated by the renewal upheavals.

In 1954 the Oakland Citizens' Committee for Urban Renewal (OCCUR) endorsed a 200-acre renewal project for West Oakland called Acorn. OCCUR did not ask for representation from the residents of West Oakland despite the fact that the Acorn project would demolish 333 buildings and force over 9,000 people to move from downtown West Oakland. The area lost further housing units to construction projects, such as the Nimitz freeway completed in 1958, BART which destroyed one side of the commercial strip along Seventh Street, and the huge postal processing center at Seventh and Wood Streets. By 1961, Oakland established a relocation office to help aid people displaced by construction and housing renewal projects.

West Oakland did not suffer by itself the housing attrition of the 1950s and 1960s. Berkeley's low-income housing project at

Codornices Village closed in 1955 when neither the city of Berkeley nor the University of California would accept responsibility for it after the emergency federal housing authority expired. Approximately 8,000 people were evicted from Codornices Village, and three-fourths of those evicted were African-Americans. In Richmond similar housing attrition occurred. Although Richmond's temporary war housing units were found to be substandard in construction, large numbers of black families lived in them until over 20,000 units were demolished in the early 1950s.[37]

Richmond did create new housing outside its city limits in Parchester Village, north of Richmond at Point Pinole. This community became an all black residential area. Touted as a "Community for All Americans," Parchester Village sold 398 homes for eight to nine thousand dollars in 1949. White families who placed deposits on homes there withdrew them before moving in thereby leaving the area for black residents who formed a tight-knit community of their own. Members of Parchester Village's Veterans Wives Club purchased a house which served as the community's recreation center. Until the early 1970s Parchester Village drew a large number of black professionals to its suburbs.[38]

Unfortunately few residential areas around California's East Bay measured up to the standards of Parchester Village. On February 13, 1963, Governor Brown called upon a joint session of the California legislature to "pass legislation to eliminate discrimination in the private housing market in California." W. Byron Rumford announced the same day that he would introduce a fair housing bill, AB 1240, which had the governor's support as well as that of several civil rights organizations.[39] Knowing that Democrats were in the majority in both houses of the legislature and that Governor Brown supported the bill, many legislators were eager to add their name as sponsors of the AB 1240. On April 25, 1963, Rumford opened the arguments for the bill on the floor of the Assembly by stating that it was time California "rid itself of this insidious practice, that of housing discrimination affecting a great number of American citizens in this state." While the Assembly held hearings on the bill, the California Real Estate Association maintained that California had "no widespread discrimination" and that the state should not restrict the right of private property owners.[40] Despite the tough stance of the California Real Estate Association, the Assembly favored AB 1240 by 47 to 25 votes. The

Fair Housing Act provided for a ceiling of $500 on civil damages that could be collected if a grievant successfully wins a civil suit charging discrimination in housing.

Advocates for the bill recognized that a still tougher battle would have to be waged in the California Senate. Assigned to Luther Gibson's Committee on Governmental Efficiency and Economy, AB 1240 faced the graveyard of the Senate. Gibson and his committee members often voted as a unit against measures concerning housing and employment opportunities for nonwhites. Delaying a vote on the bill, Gibson's committee did not act upon AB 1240 during May. Vowing to remain where they were until the bill received action, members of the Congress of Racial Equality (CORE) began a sit-in at the Capitol rotunda mezzanine. On June 14, 1963, Luther Gibson announed during a hearing that his "committee will never approve a bill prohibiting discrimination in private housing."[41] He proposed an amendment that exempted single-unit dwellings not financed by FHA, VA, or CAL-VET loans only to learn that the 1959 legislation pushed through by Augustus Hawkins already covered publicly financed housing. Adjourning without giving a new hearing date, Gibson met with Assembly Speaker Jesse Unruh and Byron Rumford to arrange a compromise. However, Rumford denounced Gibson's version of the compromise and claimed he "would prefer to discuss the matter with the full committee."[42] Finally Democratic Party leaders arranged a meeting with the members of Gibson's committee, Byron Rumford, and Governor Brown and reached an agreement to amend the bill while maintaining its enforcement powers. On the last day of the legislative session, June 21, the Committee on Governmental Efficiency and Economy sent AB 1240 to the Senate with twenty-three amendments added to it. Worried that time would elapse without a final vote, Rumford received help from liberal Democratic Senators, Joseph A. Rattigan from Sonoma and Bruce V. Regan of Los Angeles. They persuaded Gibson to bring the bill to the Senate floor where it would race against the clock for legislative acceptance. Governor Brown talked with key senators so that AB 1240 could be pushed through the Senate by a narrow margin of twenty-two to sixteen votes. This occurred at 11:00 p.m., with only one hour left before the legislative session ended. Since the Senate added twenty-three amendments to the bill, these needed to be approved by the Assembly. Five minutes before

Struggle for Legitimacy

midnight on June 21, 1963, a roll call vote began ending with 63 votes for and 15 votes opposed to the bill. Members of the Assembly and people waiting in the gallery rose to cheer Rumford as the bill passed. CORE demonstrators in the Capitol rotunda began to sing "We Shall Overcome." The Fair Housing Act, AB 1240, became law on July 18, 1963, making discrimination on account of race, color, or creed illegal when selling, renting, or leasing dwellings in California.

NOTES

1. Daniels, *Pioneer Urbanites*, 174.
2. *Ibid.*, 166.
3. *Ibid.*, 164.
4. *Ibid.*, 172.
5. *Oakland Observer*, 11 March 1944: 1. The unusual number of passengers alleged by the *Observer* to have been on board might be an indication of wartime transportation needs in the Bay Area.
6. National Maritime Union, "Discrimination Costs You Money," *Pork Chops* 32 (January 1946): 2-3.
7. *People's World*. Photograph collection, Box 6/17. Labor Archives Research Center, San Francisco, California.
8. *People's World*. Photograph Collection, Box 6/11, Labor Archives Research Center, San Francisco, California.
9. Joyce A. Henderson, Amelia Fry, Edward France, *William Bryon Rumford*, 6-7.
10. Statement on Key System by Lucie McCurry, 10 February 1945, 72/132, Cottrell L. Dellums Correspondence and Papers, Bancroft Library, University of California, Berkeley.
11. Statement on Key System by James Williams, 22 November 1944, Cottrell L. Dellums Correspondence and Papers, 72/132, Bancroft Library, University of California, Berkeley.
12. Henderson, *C.L. Dellums*, 102.
13. *Ibid.*
14. *Ibid.*, 104.
15. Henderson, *Tarea Hall Pittman*, 75.
16. California Department of Justice, Davis McEntire in collaboration with Robert B. Powers, *Police Training Bulletin: A Guide to Race Relations for Police Officers* (Sacramento: California State Printing Office, 1946).
17. *Ibid.*, 65.
18. Henderson, *C.L. Dellums*, 109.
19. Statement on the Case of Albert L. Hines, 1950, Cottrell L. Dellums Correspondence and Papers, 72/132, Bancroft Library, University of California, Berkeley.
20. Dellums claimed that "the 1946 initiative contributed greatly to the reasons it took fourteen years to get the law [the FEPC]. If the people could vote the law over, they could also vote it out. And

we would have weakened our position before the courts." Henderson, *C.L. Dellums*, 114, 115.

21. Rumford won the election with a margin of 20,387 votes. Lawrence Paul Crouchett, "Bryon Rumford: Symbol for an Era," *California History* 66 (March 1987): 15.

22. *Ibid.*, 16.

23. In June, 1962, President John F. Kennedy appointed the President's Committee on Equal Opportunity in the Armed Forces and directed it "to improve equality of opportunity for members of the Armed Forces and their dependents in the civilian community, particularly with respect to housing, education, transportation, recreational facilities, community events, programs and activities." This committee received its name as the Gesell Committee from its chairman, Gerhard A. Gesell. Richard Dalfiume, *Desegregation of the U.S. Armed Forces: Fighting on Two Fronts, 1939-1953* (Columbia, Missouri: University of Missouri Press, 1969), 222-223.

24. The African-American units in Los Angeles and San Francisco resisted integration before Rumford introduced his bill in 1949 because they feared the loss of rank if they were integrated into white units. Henderson, Fry, France, *William Bryon Rumford*, 42.

25. *Ibid.*, 17.

26. *Ibid.*, 126.

27. *Ibid.*, 121.

28. Cottrell L. Dellums Correspondence and Papers, 72/132. Bancroft Library, University of California, Berkeley.

29. Don Thomas, "Fair Employment Bill Wins Hurdle in Assembly," *Oakland Tribune*, 21 April 1955, 2(E).

30. "FEP Passes," *Oakland Tribune*, 22 April 1955, 3.

31. After the FEP bill passed in 1959, Dellums and Bill Becker, executive secretary for the California FEP Committee tallied over $100,000 as the amount spent on the committee's campaign to pass the FEP bill. *Ibid.*, 128.

32. *Ibid.*, 123.

33. *Ibid.*, 123-124. Tarea Pittman recalled that as a lobbyist for the FEPC she spoke several times to Hugh Burns and Luther Gibson in 1959. They believed that a fair employment practices act was unconstitutional and should only be implemented on a voluntary basis by employers. According to Pittman, both men "were

very hostile when you met them, very hostile!" Henderson, *Tarea Pittman*, 99-100.

34. Henderson, *C.L. Dellums*, 125.

35. Pittman said that "It is hard to believe in the backdrop of how really liberal Governor Warren became, particularly when he went on the bench, but he was not liberal at that time. He grew to be very liberal and to have a very good understanding of the proscriptions and the difficulties the minority groups were having in connection with employment." Henderson, *Tarea Hall Pittman*, 97, 108.

36. Henderson, *Tarea Hall Pittman*, 56-58.

37. Crouchett, Bunch, and Winnacker, *Visions Toward Tomorrow*, 56.

38. *Ibid.*, 56-57.

39. Crouchett, "Assemblyman W. Byron Rumford: Symbol for an Era," *California History* 66, (March 1987): 20.

40. *Ibid.*

41. *Ibid.* Rumford believed the strategy of Gibson's committee (referred to by Rumford as "this star chamber session") was to pass the bill out to the floor knowing that the senate had a long agenda pending and probably would not be able to deliberate on AB 1240 before its adjournment. Henderson, Fry, France, *William Bryon Rumford*, 118.

42. *Ibid.*

CHAPTER VI

EPILOGUE

Despite the jubilant cheers at the passage of AB 1240, opposition to the Fair Housing Act did not fade after its legislative passage. The California Real Estate Association, the Apartment House Owners Association, the California Chamber of Commerce, and State Senator John G. Schmitz of Orange County denounced the bill for promoting "forced-housing." This claim convinced many people throughout the state that the new housing legislation should be overturned. Since several states were considering fair housing legislation at this time, Assemblyman Rumford believed opponents of the Fair Housing Act desired to make California a precedent-setting example against such legislation.[1] A proposal to bring the issue of Fair Housing legislation to a popular vote received the Real Estate Association's opposition. Instead, the Real Estate Association preferred an initiative proposition binding all future legislatures through an amendment to the State Constitution. This initiative prohibited legislation against discrimination in housing. Over six hundred thousand California citizens signed a petition placing such an initiative, Proposition 14, on the November, 1964, ballot. Proposition 14 sought not only to reverse the Fair Housing Act but also to bar any locality within the state from adopting fair housing legislation. The coalition for Proposition 14 regarded the stipulation which prevented localities from passing their own fair housing laws necessary because the Berkeley City Council had passed a Fair Housing Law. The California Real Estate Association succeeded in overturning the council's action by a referendum vote, Measure C, in April, 1963.[2] The Association regarded the state proposition as a way of settling the issue presented by municipal legislation.

When a court effort, led by the NAACP and other civil rights organizations, failed to keep Proposition 14 off the ballot, California's voters were barraged by a campaign which likened "forced housing" legislation to the abridgment of fundamental private property rights. Rumford and the California Committee on Fair Practices filed an injunction petition with the State Court of Appeals questioning the constitutionality of Proposition 14 only to have their plea rejected by Judge Irving H. Perluss. Concern spread among opponents of Proposition 14 that the wording of the proposition on the ballot, "No on 14" or "Yes on 14," would confuse many potential opponents of the initiative. Rumford believed that people would think they were supporting fair housing if they voted "yes."[3] The California Federation of Labor came out against Proposition 14 as well as most church groups throughout the state. Yet on November 3, 1964, only 2.4 million Californians opposed Proposition 14 at the polls while 4.5 million citizens approved it. When the initiative passed almost two to one, African-American communities suffered one of their greatest disillusionments in the long struggle to achieve equality and legitimacy in California.

Several generations of black Californians had worked hard to create the political organizations they needed in order to achieve equality of treatment within the state. They believed they were creating a place for themselves in the California Dream; yet, the vote on Proposition 14 clearly showed them that statewide popular sentiment ran against them. Frustration within California's African-American communities ran high in the mid-1960s partially as a result of the disappointment over Proposition 14's victory.

Rumford's fair housing coalition appealed to the California Supreme Court claiming that Proposition 14 denied equal protection of the laws which the Fourteenth Amendment to the U.S. Constitution guaranteed. On May 10, 1966, the State Supreme Court declared Proposition 14 unconstitutional and reinstated the Fair Housing Act. The opponents of fair housing legislation then appealed to the U.S. Supreme Court in the case of *Reitman et al. v. Lincoln W. Mulkey*; however, the U.S. Supreme Court on May 29, 1967, upheld the 1966 decision of the California Supreme Court when it stated that the Civil Rights Act of 1866 barred discrimination in the selling or buying of property. One hundred years had lapsed since the passage of the Civil Rights Act of 1866; yet, African-Americans in California had not been protected under that law during the intervening century. Lawrence Crouchett in his biographical article on William Byron Rumford stated that "The Fair Housing Act, adopted by the legislature, repudiated by a two-

Epilogue

to-one majority of the electorate, and upheld by two high courts, marked the culmination of a generation of civil rights efforts."[4]

This comment is significant because it clearly describes the power which legislative action by African-American and, on occasion, white civil rights activists ultimately had upon California politics. Yet, despite acknowledging that he would undertake the Fair Housing campaign again if necessary, Rumford concluded in 1973 that:

> I do not think, however, that putting a law on the books is the ultimate solution to solving some of the grave problems which face us as a social group here in this country. But I would say that if people were allowed to move freely, to live as they so choose in this state of ours and in the nation, there would be no need for busing, which is only a method whereby an intercultural exposition can take place.
>
> So denying one the simple right to buy property and the right to live where he so chooses has created problems by those who attempt to foment and to continue a system of discrimination against people for what they look like, for what they are, or for what their religion happens to be.[5]

The shift from reliance upon legislative redress for inequalities facing African-Americans indicated how quickly the frustration over Proposition 14's victory and the increasing radicalism of California's East Bay after 1963 influenced the thought of even moderate spokespeople for legal change such as Rumford.

As skepticism regarding the achievement of equality and legitimacy through legal processes grew among the African-American community so, too, did the California Dream falter for many in the East Bay. Integration for African-Americans into California's dominant white society still remained an elusive goal in the years after 1963. Cautionary warnings in African-American editorials during the 1860s appeared to be as valid a century later as they had been when they were first made.

Editorials in both the *Elevator* and the *Pacific Appeal* maintained that separate institutions were necessary for the protection of the state's African-American minority.

> ... in all our communities there are separate and distinct social relations which no law can rule or govern, nor is it desirable they should. This is one of the attributes of our present high state of civilization, and it marks the progress of the human race. [If Blacks abandon their separate institutions], where will we go? ... [American] social interests are distinct, and on these grounds require separate organizations.... Until we can separate ourselves from the race with which we are identified, and each one can unite with the class with which we affiliate by education, fortune, and other adventitious circumstances, we must maintain our separate organizations; and to keep up a unity of thought, feeling, and interest, frequent deliberation is necessary.[6]

These separate institutions presented African-Americans in the East Bay with a paradox that began to appear to many, such as Assemblyman Rumford, too complex to unravel by legislation alone.

Nathan Huggins, in his preface to *Pioneer Urbanites*, guages the depth of that paradox when he remarked that:

> to become part of the mainstream one would minimize racial identity, submerge difference, become invisible; but to gain the power and political leverage to demand fair treatment and respect, one needed conspicuous numbers and racial identity.[7]

The legislative and communal associations which African-American communities in the East Bay built from 1850 to 1963 parallel their counterparts in California's white society. However, the statewide strength of groups opposed to the Rumford Fair Housing Act provided many African-Americans with a foreboding that political and social equality might still be far from reach in California.

East Bay leaders would directly confront this paradox as they grappled with their desire for legitimacy within the white community as well as their desire for the racial identification and pride which the Black Power Movement defined in the latter part of the 1960s.

What becomes increasingly apparent during this decade is that a transition in leadership within the African-American communities accompanied the growing radicalism of African-Americans in California. Unlike the struggle between African-American migrants to California in World War II and the already established black

Epilogue 155

residents of the East Bay, the political frustrations and radical changes in attitude of African-Americans in the 1960s (often portrayed as a generational conflict) resulted in a change of leadership as well as a change in political strategy.[8]

Although the earlier "pioneer urbanite" leaders of the East Bay remained active during the 1960s, change did occur. Nothing reveals the extent of that change so much as the community ethos of the Black Power movement after 1966. Even the music of the decade reflected that change as the rhythm and blues music of the 1940s and 1950s is replaced by Soul. Richard Maxwell Brown comments that:

> Soul, too, was a prideful concept, for those deemed lacking in soul—whites, of course, but also upper- and middle-class blacks stained by the accretion of particular white cultural traits—were considered inferior. The very term 'soul,' in drawing upon the strong religiosity of the black masses itself, arrogated to its possessors alone, as it were, the fully human quality. By implication those without Soul were 'somewhat less human.'[9]

This concept of black pride, "soul," began to permeate African-American communities during the latter part of the 1960s.

Black pride fed upon a sense of unique African-American identity, rather than acculturalization within the dominant white community. This became the new direction which youthful Black Power leaders began to stress in California's East Bay. Yet their programs and demands were tempered and based within the century-old quest for the freedoms and equality expressed in the concept of the California Dream. New directions and strategies developed throughout the 1960s; however, the political and economic achievements of the years from 1850 to 1963 still remained the cornerstone of the African-American communities of California's East Bay.

NOTES

1. Henderson, Fry, France, *William Bryon Rumford*, 120.
2. *Ibid.*, 115.
3. *Ibid.*, 125.
4. Crouchett, "Assemblyman W. Byron Rumford," 22.
5. Henderson, Fry, France, *William Bryon Rumford*, 129.
6. Daniels, *Pioneer Urbanites*, 110.
7. *Ibid.*, xii.
8. The struggle between World War II newcomers and the earlier African-American residents of the East Bay did not result in a change of leadership so much as a melding of the demands of the newcomers with the strategies for political and economic legitimacy which earlier African-American leaders had created. Shirley Ann Moore, "Getting There, Being There: Afro-American Migration to Richmond, California," Paper presented at the Western History Association Conference, Sparks, Nevada, 19 October 1990.
9. Brown, *Strain of Violence*, 228.

BIBLIOGRAPHY

PARALLEL COMMUNITIES: AFRICAN-AMERICANS IN CALIFORNIA'S EAST BAY, 1850-1963

The following bibliography contains all the items cited in the notes to the text as well as many items which were of value in the preparation of this study but which do not appear in the notes.

I. Primary sources, unprinted
    A. Public records
    B. Journals, letters, and papers of private individuals
    C. Oral history interviews

II. Primary sources, printed
    A. Public records
    B. Letters, pamphlets, and papers of private individuals
    C. Newspapers and magazines
    D. Oral history interviews

III. Secondary works
    A. Books, monographs, pamphlets
    B. Articles
    C. Unpublished theses

I. PRIMARY SOURCES, UNPRINTED

A. Public records

American Civil Liberties Union. Northern California. Boxes 17, 27-28. California Historical Society, San Francisco.

California. Legislature. Assembly. Committee on Government Efficiency and Economy. Rumford Fair Housing Act: Proposed Bills, Amendments; Newspaper Clippings; Background materials and data concerning the passage of Prop. 14, Rumford Act, and subsequent amendments. Period covers 1959-1968, 1/2 cu. ft. California State Archives, Sacramento.

United States. Department of Justice. Federal Surveillance of Afro-Americans, 1917-1925: The First World War, the Red Scare and the Garvey Movement. Black Studies Research Sources. Microfilm from major archival and manuscript collections. Ann Arbor, Michigan: University Publications of America, 1986.

B. *Journals, letters, and papers of private individuals*

Albrier, Frances Mary. Correspondence and Papers, Scrapbook. Bancroft Library, University of California, Berkeley.

Dellums, Cottrell L. Correspondence and Papers. Cartons 4-9, 19, 21, 23, 25, 40. Bancroft Library, University of California, Berkeley.

Kaiser, Henry J. Correspondence and Papers. Period covering 1930-1960. Bancroft Library, University of California, Berkeley.

C. *Oral history interviews*

Coleman II, Edwin Leon. Interview by author. 11 May 1990. Eugene, Oregon. Tape Recording.

Crouchett, Lawrence P. Interview by author. 3 August, 1989. Oakland, California. Telephone Conversation.

II. PRIMARY SOURCES, PRINTED

A. *Public records*

Address of the State Executive Committee to the Colored People of the Colored People of the State of California. Sacramento, 1859.

Berkeley. Citizen's Committee to Study Discrimination in Housing. *Appendix to Report of Citizen's Committee to Study Discrimination in Housing in Berkeley.* Berkeley, California: 1962.

California. Department of Industrial Relations, Division of Fair Employment Practices. *Negro Californians: Population, Employment, Income, and Education.* San Francisco, June 1963; reprint, April 1967.

California. Department of Justice. Davis McEntire and Robert B. Powers. *Police Training Bulletin: A Guide to Race Relations for Police Officers.* Sacramento: California State Printing Office, 1946.

California. Governor's Commission on the Rumford Act. *Report of the Governor's Commission on the Rumford Act.* Sacramento: California State Printing Office, 1967.

California. Legislature. House. *Journal.* 1st Session.

California. Legislature. Senate. *Journal.* 16th Session.

_____. *Journal.* 19th Session.

California. Secretary of State. *Certified Abstract of the Statement of the Vote Polled in Alameda County, California, Relating to Votes Given for Governor and Lieutenant Governor, at the General Election, November, 1934.* Sacramento: California State Archives, 1934.

James et al. v. Marinship Corporation. 25, 721, 2nd California Reports, 1944.

Kerns, J. Harvey. *Study of Social and Economic Conditions Affecting the Local Negro Population*. Oakland: Council of Social Agencies and Community Chest, 1942.

President's Committee on Civil Rights. *To Secure These Rights*. Washington, D.C.: Government Printing Office, 1947.

Proceedings of the First State Convention of the Colored Citizens of the State of California. 1855, 1856, 1865. Sacramento: Democratic State Journal Print, 1855; reprint, San Francisco: R & E Research Associations, 1969.

Restrictions by Federal Housing Administration for SheffieldVillage, 10 March 1939 [on exhibit at Oakland Museum, February 1989].

Tilghman, Charles F., comp. *Colored Directory of the Leading Cities of Northern California, 1916-1917*. Oakland, 1917.

United States. Commission on Civil Rights. *Hearings: Housing*. Washington, D.C.: Government Printing Office, 1959.

United States. Congress. House. A *Bill to Prevent the Enlistment of Negroes in the Military Service of the United States*, H.R. 17183 64th Congress, 1st session, 1916.

_____. Committee on Appropriations. Department of Labor. Hearings *before the Subcommittee of the Committee on Washington*. 76th Congress, 1940.

United States. Congress. Senate. Committee on Appropriations. Supplemental Appropriation Bill for 1936. *Hearings before the Subcommittee of the Committee on Appropriations*. 74th Congress, 1936.

_____. Committee on Education and Labor. *Hearings on the Fair Employment Practices Act*. 78th Congress, 1944

United States. *Special Census of Oakland, California, October 9, 1945*. Washington, D.C., 1946.

United States. *Twelfth Census, 1900*: *Population*, I: 18, II: 77-72. Washington, D.C.

United States. *Thirteenth Census, 1910*: *Population*, II: 180. Washington, D.C.

United States. *Fourteenth Census, 1920*: *Population*. Washington, D.C.

United States. *Fifteenth Census, 1930*: *Population*, II: 115. Washington, D.C.

United States. *Sixteenth Census, 1940*: *Housing*, I. Washington, D.C.

_____. *Sixteenth Census, 1940*: *Population*, I. Washington, D.C., 1943.

United States. *Seventeenth Census, 1950*: *Population*. Washington, D.C.

United States. *Eighteenth Census, 1960*: *Population*. Washington, D.C.

B. *Letters, pamphlets, and papers of private individuals*

Hill, Robert A., ed. *The Marcus Garvey and Universal Negro Improvement Association Papers* 4 (1 September 1921- 2 September 1922). Berkeley and Los Angeles: University of California Press, 1985.

Maritime Federation of the Pacific. *Records, 1935-1945*. Labor Archives and Research Center, San Francisco State University, San Francisco.

People's World. Photograph Collection. Labor Archives and Research Center, San Francisco State University, San Francisco.

San Francisco Labor Council. *Records, 1902-1976*. Labor Archives and Research Center, San Francisco State University, San Francisco.

Wall's Addition to the City of Richmond, Pamphlet 4599-45 [on exhibit at Oakland Northern California Center for Afro-American History and Life].

C. *Newspapers and magazines*

University of California, Berkeley:

Alta California (San Francisco), 1867.

California Voice (Oakland), 1919- [fragments].

Californian (San Francisco), 1849.

Crisis, 12-18, 1916-1919; 50, 1943.

Elevator (San Francisco), 1865-1898.

Fore'n'Aft (Richmond), Vols. 4-5, in the Henry J. KaiserCollection, Bancroft Library, University of California, Berkeley.

Independent (Oakland), 1929-1931.

Labor Clarion, v. 16-25, February 9, 1917-January 28, 1927; 1930-1934 [fragments].

Messenger, 1919-1920 [fragments].

Mirror of the Times (San Francisco), 22 August 1857; 12 December 1857.

Observer (Oakland), 1944.

Pacific Appeal (San Francisco), 1862-1879.

Pacific Coast Appeal (San Francisco), 1898-1925.

San Francisco Examiner, 1867-1990 [fragments].

San Francisco News, 1939.

Bibliography

Seamen's Journal, 1936 [fragments].

Sunshine (Oakland), 1900-1923.

Times (Oakland), 1923-1930.

Tribune (Oakland), 1940-1955.

Western American (Oakland), 1926-1929.

Western Appeal (San Francisco), 1918 [fragments]-1927.

Western Outlook (Oakland), 1894-1924.

Labor Archives and Research Center, San Francisco State University:

People's World (San Francisco), 1944-1965 [fragments].

Pork Chops, 32 (1946, fragments).

D. *Oral history interviews*

Chall, Malca. *Frances Mary Albrier: Determined Advocate for Racial Equality*. Berkeley, California: Regional Oral History Office, Bancroft Library, 1973.

Henderson, Joyce. *C. L. Dellums: International President of the Brotherhood of Sleeping Car Porters and Civil Rights Leader*. Berkeley, California: Regional Oral History Office, Bancroft Library, 1973.

_____. *Tarea Hall Pittman: NAACP Official and Civil Rights Worker*. Berkeley, California: Regional Oral History Office, Bancroft Library, 1974.

_____, Amelia Fry, and Edward France. *William Byron Rumford: Legislator for Fair Employment, Fair Housing, and Public Health*. Berkeley, California: Regional Oral History Office, Bancroft Library, 1973.

Stanford University Radio Station KZSU, *Project South Oral History Collection*, Microfilming Corporation of America, 1975. Covers ten weeks of interviews collected by eight recorders throughout the South during 1964.

III. SECONDARY WORKS

A. *Books, pamphlets, monographs*

Abajian, James de T. *Blacks and Their Contributions to the American West; A Bibliography and Union List of Library Holdings Through 1970.* Boston: G. K. Hall, 1974.

──────. *Blacks in Selected Newspapers, Censuses and Other Sources: An Index to Names and Subjects*, 3 vols., 2 vols. supplement. Boston: G. K. Hall & Co., 1977.

Allen, Robert L. *The Port Chicago Mutiny: The Story of the Largest Mass Mutiny Trial in U.S. Naval History* (New York: Warner Books, Inc., 1989).

Anderson, Jervis. *A. Philip Randolph: A Biographical Portrait.* New York: Harcourt Brace Jovanovich, Inc., 1972.

Archibald, Katherine. *Wartime Shipyard: A Study of Social Disunity.* Berkeley and Los Angeles: University of California Press, 1947.

Bancroft, Hubert Howe. *History of the Pacific States of North America*, II, *California*. San Francisco: A. L. Bancroft & Co., 1885.

Beasley, Delilah L. *The Negro Trail Blazers of California.* Los Angeles: 1919; reprint, San Francisco: R and E Research Associates, 1968.

Beck, Warren A. and David A. Williams. *California: A History of the Golden State.* Garden City, New York: Doubleday & Company, Inc., 1972.

Berwanger, Eugene H. *The Frontier Against Slavery: Western Anti-Negro Prejudice and the Slavery Extension Controversy.* Urbana, Illinois: University of Illinois Press, 1967.

Bloom, Jack M. *Class, Race, & the Civil Rights Movement.* Bloomington and Indianapolis: Indiana University Press, 1987.

Blum, John Morton. *V Was for Victory: Politics and American Culture During World War II*. New York: Harcourt Brace Jovanovich, 1976.

Borthwick, J. D. *Three Years in California*. London, 1857; reprint, Oakland, 1948.

Branch, Taylor. *Parting the Waters: America in the King Years 1954-63*. New York: Simon and Shuster, 1988.

Brown, Richard Maxwell. *Strain of Violence: Historical Studies of American Violence and Vigilantism*. New York: Oxford University Press, 1977.

Carson, Claybourne, Jr.. *In Struggle: SNCC and the Black Awakening of the 1960s*. Cambridge: Harvard University Press, 1981.

Casstevens, Thomas W. *Politics, Housing and Race Relations: California's Rumford Act and Proposition 14*. 1967.

Cross, Ira Brown. *A History of the Labor Movement in California*. Berkeley: University of California Press, 1935; reprint, University of California Press, 1974.

Crouchett, Lawrence P, Lonnie G. Bunch,III, and Martha Kendall Winnacker. *Visions Toward Tomorrow: The History of the East Bay Afro-American Community 1852-1977*. Oakland: Northern California Center for Afro-American History and Life, 1989.

Dalfiume, Richard M. *Desegregation of the U.S. Armed Forces: Fighting on Two Fronts, 1939-1953*. Columbia, Missouri: University of Missouri Press, 1969.

Daniels, Douglas Henry. *Pioneer Urbanites: A Social and Cultural History of Black San Francisco*. Philadelphia: Temple University Press, 1980.

Drake, St. Clair and Horace R. Cayton. *Black Metropolis: A Study of Negro Life in a Northern City*, 2 vols. New York: Harcourt,

Brace, 1945; reprinted., New York: Harper & Row, Harper Torchbooks, 1962.

Dunne, William F. *The Great San Francisco General Strike*; *The Story of the West Coast Strike - the Bay Counties General Strike and the Maritime Workers Strike*. New York: Workers Library, 1934.

Foner, Philip S., and Ronald L. Lewis, eds., *The Era of Post-War Prosperity and the Great Depression, 1920-1936*, vol. 6, *The Black Worker: A Documentary History from Colonial Times to the Present*. Philadelphia: Temple University Press, 1981.

Frakes, George E. and Curtis B. Solberg, eds. *Minorities in California History*. New York: Random House, 1971.

Fredrickson, George. *The Black Image in the White Mind*: *The Debate on the Afro-American Character and Destiny, 1817-1914*. New York: Harper & Row, 1972.

Frost, Richard H. *The Mooney Case*. Stanford: Stanford University Press, 1968.

Garfinkel, Herbert. *When Negroes March*: *The March on Washington Movement in the Organizational Politics for FEPC*. Glencoe, Illinois: The Free Press, 1959.

Gelfand, Mark I. *A Nation of Cities*: *The Federal Government and Urban America, 1933-1965*. New York: Oxford University Press, 1975.

Goode, Kenneth G. *California's Black Pioneers: A Brief Historical Survey*. Santa Barbara, California: McNally & Loftin, Publishers, 1974.

Gossett, Thomas F. *Race: The History of an Idea in America*. New York: Schocken Books, 1965.

Graham, Hugh Davis and Ted Robert Gurr, eds. *Violence in America: Historical and Comparative Perspectives*. New York: New American Library, 1969.

Grimshaw, Allen D., ed. *Racial Violence in the United States*. Chicago: Aldine Publishing Company, 1969.

Grossman, James R. *Land of Hope: Chicago Black Southerners, and the Great Migration*. Chicago: University of Chicago Press, 1989.

Harris, William H. *The Harder We Run, Black Workers Since the Civil War*. New York: Oxford University Press, 1982.

Haynes, Robert V. *A Night of Violence: The Houston Riot of 1917*. Baton Rouge: Louisiana State University Press, 1976.

Hine, Darlene Clark, ed. *The State of Afro-American History: Past Present, and Future*. Baton Rouge: Louisiana State University Press, 1986.

Hirsch, Arnold R. *Making the Second Ghetto: Race and Housing in Chicago, 1940-1960*. Cambridge: Cambridge University Press, 1983.

Hittell, Theodore H. *History of California* 4. San Francisco: N. J. Stone & Co., 1897.

Holdredge, Helen. *Mammy Pleasant*. New York: G. P. Putnam's Sons, 1953.

Holli, Melvin G. and Peter d'A. Jones. *The Ethnic Frontier:Essays in the History of Group Survival in Chicago and the Midwest*. Grand Rapids, Mich.: Eerdmans, 1977.

Hunter, Floyd. *Housing Discrimination in Oakland*. Berkeley: Floyd Hunter Co., 1964.

Issel, William and Robert W. Cherney. *San Francisco, 1865-1932: Politics, Power, and Urban Development*. Berkeley, Los Angeles, and London: University of California Press, 1986.

Jackson, Kenneth T. *Crabgrass Frontier: The Suburbanization of America*. New York: Oxford University Press, 1987.

Johnson, Charles S. *The Negro War Worker in San Francisco: A Local Self-Survey*. San Francisco: Y.W.C.A., 1944.

Jones, Landon Y. *Great Expectations: America and the Baby Boom Generation*. New York: Ballantine, 1980.

Jordan, Winthrop D. *White Over Black: American Attitudes Toward the Negro 1550-1812*. Baltimore: Pelican Books, 1969.

Katzman, David M. *Before the Ghetto: Black Detroit in the Nineteenth Century*. Urbana: University of Illinois Press, 1973.

King, Jr. Martin Luther. *Why We Can't Wait*. New York: Signet Book, 1963.

Kip, Leonard. *California Sketches with Recollections of the Gold Mines*. Los Angeles: 1946.

Kusmer, Kenneth L. *A Ghetto Takes Shape: Black Cleveland, 1870-1930*. Urbana: University of Illinois Press, 1976.

Lapp, Rudolph M. *Blacks in Gold Rush California*. New Haven and London: Yale University Press, 1977.

Levine, Lawrence, *Black Culture and Black Consciousness: Afro-American Thought From Slavery to Freedom*. New York: Oxford University Press, 1977.

Limerick, Patricia Nelson. *The Legacy of Conquest*. New York: W. W. Norton & Company, 1987.

Litwack, Leon F. *North of Slavery: The Negro in the Free States, 1790-1860*. Chicago: University of Chicago Press, 1961.

McLagan, Elizabeth. *A Peculiar Paradise: A History of Blacks in Oregon, 1788-1940*. Portland, Oregon: Georgian Press Company, 1980.

Malone, Michael P. and Richard W. Etulain. *The American West: A Twentieth Century West*. Lincoln: University of Nebraska Press, 1989.

Meier, August and Elliott Rudwick. *Black History and the Historical Profession, 1915-1980*. Urbana: University of Illinois Press, 1986.

———. *Black Protest in the Sixties*. Chicago: Quandrangle Books, 1970.

———. *CORE: A Study in the Civil Rights Movement*. Urbana: University of Illinois Press, 1975.

———. *The Making of Black America; Essays in Negro Life and History*. New York: Atheneum, 1969.

———, eds. *Federal Surveillance of Afro-Americans, 1917-1925: The First World War, the Red Scare and the Garvey Movement*. Black Studies Research Sources. Guide to microfilm collection. Ann Arbor, Michigan: University Publications of America, 1986.

Montesano, Phil. *The Black Churches in Urban San Francisco, 1860-1865: Their Educational, Civic, and Civil Rights Activities*. c. 1968?

Muller, William G. *The Twenty-Fourth Infantry, Past and Present* (privately printed, 1922).

Myrdal, Gunnar. *An American Dilemma*, 2 Vols. New York: Harper & Row, 1962.

Nash, Gerald D. *The American West in the Twentieth Century: A Short History of an Urban Oasis*. Englewood Cliffs, New Jersey: Prentice-Hall, Inc., 1973.

———. *The American West Transformed: The Impact of the Second World War*. Bloomington: University of Indiana, 1985.

Novak, Michael. *The Rise of the Unmeltable Ethnics*. New York: Macmillan, 1973.

Olmsted, Roger R. *Scow Schooners of San Francisco Bay*. Edited by Nancy Olmsted. Cupertino, CA: California History Center, 1988.

_____, and Charles Wollenberg, eds. *Neither Separate nor Equal: Race and Racism in California*. San Francisco: California Historical Society, 1971.

Osofsky, Gilbert. *Harlem: The Making of a Ghetto; Negro New York, 1890-1930*. New York: Harper & Row, 1966.

Philpott, Thomas L. *The Slum and the Ghetto: Neighborhood Deterioration and Middle-Class Reform, Chicago, 1880-1930*. New York: Oxford University Press, 1978.

Pinner, Frank A. *Old Age and Political Behavior; A CaseStudy*. Berkeley: University of California Press, 1959.

Porter, Kenneth Wiggins. *The Negro on the American Frontier*. New York: Arno Press, 1971.

Rice, Richard B., William A. Bullough, and Richard J. Orsi. *The Elusive Eden: A New History of California*. New York: Alfred A. Knopf, 1988.

Roper, John Herbert. *C. Vann Woodward, Southerner*. Athens, GA and London: The University of Georgia Press, 1987.

Ruchames, Louis. *Race, Jobs, & Politics: The Story of FEPC*. New York: Columbia University Press, 1953.

Santino, Jack. *Miles of Smiles, Years of Struggle*. Urbana and Chicago: University of Illinois Press, 1989.

Savage, William Sherman. *Blacks in the West*. Westport, CN: Greenwood Press, 1976.

Saxton. Alexander. *The Indispensable Enemy: Labor and the Anti-Chinese Movement in California.* Berkeley and Los Angeles: University of California Press, 1971.

Scott, Emmett J. *American Negro in the World War.* Chicago: L. W. Walters Co., 1919.

Sitkoff, Harvard. *The Struggle for Black Equality, 1954-1980.* New York: Hill and Wang, 1966.

Spear, Allan H. *Black Chicago: The Making of a Negro Ghetto, 1890-1920.* Chicago: University of Chicago Press, 1967.

Starr, Kevin. *Americans and the California Dream, 1850-1915.* New York: Oxford University Press, 1973.

Trotter, Joe William, Jr.. *Black Milwaukee, The Making of an Industrial Proletariat, 1915-45.* Urbana: University of Illinois Press, 1985.

Tuttle, Jr., William M. *Race Riot: Chicago in the Red Summer of 1919.* New York: Atheneum, 1974.

Unger, Irwin. *The Movement: A History of the New American Left, 1959-1972.* New York: University Press of America, 1974.

Vandiver, Frank E. *Black Jack: The Life and Times of John J. Pershing*, Vol. 2. College Station, Tx and London: Texas A & M University, 1977.

Walls, Dwayne W. *Chicken Bone Special.* New York: Harcourt, Brace Jovanovich, Inc., 1973.

Watkins, Walter F. *The Cry of the West: The Story of the Mighty Struggle for Religious Freedom in California.* San Francisco: 1925; reprint, R & E Research Associates: 1969.

Weaver, Robert C. *The Negro Ghetto.* New York: Harper & Row, 1948.

Wilson, James Q. *Negro Politics: The Search for Leadership*. New York: Free Press, 1960.

Wirt, Frederick M. *Power in the City: Decision Making in San Francisco*. Berkeley: University of California Press, 1974.

Wollenberg, Charles, ed. *Ethnic Conflict in California History*. Los Angeles: Tinnon-Brown, Inc., Book Publishers, 1970.

Woodson, Carter G. *A Century of Negro Migration*. Washington, D.C., 1918; reprint, New York: AMS Press, Inc., 1970.

Wright, George C. *Life Behind a Veil: Blacks in Louisville, Kentucky, 1865-1930*. Baton Rouge: Louisiana State University Press, 1985.

Wye, Christopher. "The New Deal and the Negro Community: Toward a Broader Conceptualization." *Journal of American History* 59 (December 1972): 621-639.

Zinn, Howard. *SNCC: The New Abolitionists*. Boston: Beacon Press, 1964.

B. *Articles*

"Absolute Discretion? The California Controversy over Fair Housing Laws." *Interracial Review* 38 (Oct. 1965): 155-181ff.

Barger, Bob. "Raymond L. Haight and the Commonwealth Progessive Campaign of 1934." *California Historical Society Quarterly* 43 (September 1964): 219-230.

Barley, J. "Oakland Presents Its Case for Salvaging a Ghetto." *Architectural Forum* 126 (Apr. 1967): 42-45.

Bell, Howard Holman. "Negroes in California, 1849-1859." *Phylon* 28 (Summer, 1967): 151-60.

Bellisfield, Gwen. "White Attitudes Toward Racial Integration and the Urban Riots of 1960s." *The Public Opinion Quarterly* 36 (Winter, 1972/73): 579-584.

Bolster, W. Jeffrey. "'To Feel like a Man': Black Seamen in the Northern States, 1800-1860," *Journal of American History* 76 (March 1990): 1173-1199.

Brechin, Gray. "Sailing to Byzantium: The Architecture of the Panama Pacific International Exposition," *California Historical Quarterly* 62 (Summer 1983): 106-121.

Broussard, Albert S. "Organizing the Black Community in the San Francisco Bay Area, 1915-1930," *Arizona and the West* 23 (Winter, 1981).

_____. "Strange Territory, Familiar Leadership: The Impact of World War II on San Francisco's Black Community," *California History* 65 (March 1986): 18-25.

Colbert, Robert E. "Current Trends and Events [Section C]: The Attitude of Older Negro Residents Toward Recent Negro Migrants in the Pacific Northwest." *Journal of Negro Education* 15 (Fall 1946): 695-703.

Converse, Philip E. "Comment: The Status of Nonattitudes." *The American Political Science Review* 68 (1974): 650-660.

Crespi, Irving. "Racial Attitudes of Whites in Politics and Education." *The Public Opinion Quarterly*, 38 (Fall 1974): 422.

Crouchett, Lawrence P. "Assemblyman W. Byron Rumford: Symbol for an Era." *California History* 66 (March 1987): 12-23.

_____. "The 'Forgotten Years' of the Negro Revolution."*Journal of American History* 55 (June 1968): 90-106.

Degler, Carl. "The Negro in America--Where Myrdal Went Wrong." *New York Times Magazine* (December 7, 1969): 644ff.

DuBois, W. E. B. "An Essay Toward a History of the Black Man in the Great War," *The Crisis* 18 (June 1919).

Dyer, Brainerd. "One Hundred Years of Negro Suffrage." *Pacific Historical Review* 37 (February 1968): 1-20.

Edwards, Malcolm. "The War of Complexional Distinction: Blacks in Gold Rush California & British Columbia," *California Historical Quarterly* 66 (Spring 1977): 34-45.

"Explorations in Black Maritime History Exhibit." *Maritime Humanities Newsletter* 2 (Spring 1983).

Fisher, James A., "The Political Development of the Black Community in California, 1850-1950," *California Historical Quarterly* 50 (September 1971): 256-266.

Forbes, Jack D. "Black Pioneers: The Spanish-Speaking Afro-Americans of the Southwest," *Phylon* 27 (1966).

Franklin, John Hope. "Afro-American History: State of the Art," *Journal of American History* 75 (June 1988): 162-175.

Frye, Hardy. "Negroes in California from 1841 to 1875," *California History Series*, vol. 3 (San Francisco: San Francisco Negro Historical and Cultural Society, 1968), 4.

Gillam, Richard. "White Racism and the Civil Rights Movement." *The Yale Review*, 62 (June 1973): 520-543.

Harding, Vincent Gordon. "Wrestling toward the Dawn: The Afro-American Freedom Movement and the Changing Constitution." *The Journal of American History* 74 (December 1987): 718-739.

Hawkins, Homer C. "Trends in Black Migration from 1863-1960." *Phylon* 34 (June 1973): 140-152.

Jackson, Kenneth T. "Race, Ethnicity, and Real Estate Appraisal: The Home Owners Loan Corporation and the Federal Housing

Administration." *Journal of Urban History* 6 (August 1980): 419-452.

Jensen, Joan M. "Apartheid: Pacific Coast Style." *Pacific Historical Review* 38 (Aug. 1969): 335-340.

Jones, Faustine C. "Black Americans and the City: A Historical Survey." *The Journal of Negro Education* 62 (Summer, 1973): 261-282.

Krebs, Ottole. "The Post-War Negro in San Francisco." In *American Communities* 2. Oakland: Mills College, 1949.

Litwack, Leon F. "Obituary: Nathan Irvin Huggins." *OAH Newsletter* 18 (February 1990).

Molitar, Tony. "From Slavery to Amtrak: A History of the Pullman Porters in the East Bay." Paper presented at the Southwest Labor History Association conference, San Francisco, California, 28 April 1989.

Montesano, Philip M. "San Francisco Black Churches in the Early 1860's: Political Pressure Group." *California Historical Quarterly* 52 (Summer 1973).

Moore, Shirley Ann. "Getting There, Being There: Afro-American Migration to Richmond, California." Paper presented at the Western History Association Conference, Sparks, Nevada, 19 October 1990.

National Maritime Union. "Discrimination Costs You Money." *Pork* Chops 32 (January 1946): 2-3.

Osofsky, Gilbert. "The Enduring Ghetto." *Journal of American History* 55 (September 1968): 243-255.

Reid, John D. "Black Urbanization of the South." *Phylon* 35 (September 1974): 259-277.

"Richmond Took a Beating: From Civic Chaos Came Ships for War and Some Hope for the Future." *Fortune* 31 (February, 1945): 262-269.

Schuler, Edgar A. "The Houston Race Riot, 1917," *Journal of Negro History* 24 (July 1944), 301-338.

Schwartz, Harvey. "Harry Bridges and the Scholars Looking at History's Verdict." *California History* 59 (Spring 1980).

Selvin, David F. "Days of Rage." *San Francisco Chronicle*, 3 July 1988, A13-14.

Sitkoff, Harvard. "Racial Militancy and Inter-racial Violence in the Second World War." *Journal of American History* 55 (June 1968): 661-681.

Smith, Alonzo and Quintard Taylor. "Racial Discrimination in the Workplace: A Study of Two West Coast Cities During the 1940s." *The Journal of Ethnic History* 8 (Spring 1980): 35-54.

Snodgrass, J. William. "The Black Press in the San Francisco Bay Area, 1856-1900." *California History* 60 (Winter 1981/82): 306-317.

Stanley, John. "Search for Cause of Mysterious Explosion." *San Francisco Chronicle*, 3 June 1990, 47-48.

Taylor, Quintard. "Black Urban Development - Another View: Seattle's Central District, 1910-1940." *Pacific Historical Review* 58 (November 1989): 429-448.

_____. "The Great Migration: The Afro American Communities of Seattle and Portland During the 1940s." *Arizona and the West* 23 (1981): 105-106.

"That Riot on Twelfth Street." *Oakland Observer*, 11 March 1944, 1.

Tompkins, E. Berkeley. "Black Ahab: William T. Shorey, Whaling Master." *California Historical Quarterly* 51 (Spring 1972).

Wilkins, Roy. "The West in Wartime." *Crisis* 50 (Feb. 1943): 42-44.

Wolfinger, Raymond E. and Greenstein, Fred E. "The Repeal of Fair Housing in California: An Analysis of Referendum Voting,"*American Political Science Review* 62 (September 1968): 753-769.

Wollenberg, Charles. "Blacks vs. Navy Blue: The Mare Island Mutiny Court Martial." *California History* 58 (Spring 1979): 62-75.

_____. "James vs. Marinship: Trouble on the New Black Frontier." *California History* 60 (Fall 1981): 262-279.

C. *Unpublished theses*

Alancraig, Helen Smith. "Cordonices Village: A Study of Non-Segregated Public Housing in the San Francisco Bay Area." M.A. thesis, University of California, Berkeley, 1953.

Broussard, Albert S. "The New Racial Frontier: San Francisco's Black Community, 1900-1940." Ph.D. diss., Duke University, 1977.

France, Edward E. "Some Aspects of the Migration of the Negro to the San Francisco Bay Area Since 1940." Ph.D. diss, University of California, Berkeley, 1962.

Moore, Shirley Ann. "The Community in Richmond, California 1910-1963." Ph.D. diss., University of Minnesota, Minneapolis, 1979.

Taylor Jr., Quintard. "A History of Blacks in the Pacific Northwest, 1788-1970." Ph.D. diss., University of Minnesota, Minneapolis, 1979.

Thurman, Odell A. "The Negro in California Before 1890." M.A. thesis, College of the Pacific, 1945; reprint, San Francisco: R and E Research Associates, 1973.

INDEX

Abbott, Robert, 51n.22
Abolitionist Sentiment, 4, 26n.21
Abshire, F. Presley, 140
Acorn Club, 58
Acty, Ruth, 79
African-American Co-Operative Association, 35, 50n.13
African-Americans:
  activism, 91
  boosterism, 55, 64
  boycotts, 131
  colonization of, 46
  employment of, 33, 49
  enlistment in military, 53n.48
  exclusion practices, 17
  Federal Surveillance of, 1917-1925, 52n.34, 53n.44-45
  housing, 80, 91, 94-96
  in California, 3, 5, 6, 14, 20
  in mining, 5
  in Philippines, 32
  in prison, 6
  in union auxiliaries, 76, 105, 107, 113
  in unions, 106
  legitimacy, 11, 23, 129
  membership in ILWU, 75
  migration to British Columbia, 7
  migration to defense industry jobs, 93
  military regiment, 47
  "New Crowd," 49
  nurses, 71
  "Old Crowd," 49
  political leagues, 19
  press, 26n.26
  restrictive ordinances, 80, 97
  University of California, Berkeley students, 58
  World War II experience, 94
Agricultural Adjustment Act, 76
Alameda:
  Central Labor Council, 76
  County Supervisors, 71
  Democratic Central Committee, 78
  Highland Training Hospital, 71
  Japanese All-Stars, 64
  Labor Council, 68
  NAACP chapter formed, 61
Albany Argus, 5
Albatross, 4
Albrier, Frances, 56, 57, 60, 69, 77-78, 90n.88, 106-107, 115-116
Allen, Robert L., 116, 127n.78
Alpha Kappa Alpha Society: Rho Chapter, 58

181

Alta, 12, 17
Amalgamates Streetcar Union, 133
American Federation of Labor, 68, 105, 106, 113
Amos, James, 44
Amundsen, Spencer O., 135
Anderson, Edward, 111
Anderson, George, 113
Anderson, Jervis, 103
Anderson, T.M., 108
Angus Club, 79
Apartment House Owners Association, 151
Appomatox Club, 60
Archibald, Katherine, 108
Architect and Engineer, 41
Art and Industrial Club, 62
Asilomar, 72
Associated Farmers, 141
Associated Railroad Employees of California, 33
Atlantic Monthly, 38

Baja California, 65
Ballou, C.C., 48
Bancroft, H.H., 24n3
Baptist Church:
  Beth Eden Baptist Church, 22, 38, 56
  Ebenezer Baptist Church, 22
  First Baptist Church, 60
  New Hope Baptist Church, 22
  St. John's Baptist Church, 60
Barry, John D., 77

Beasley, Delilah, 56, 57, 83n.6
Bechtel, W.A.:
  Company, 109
  Marinship Corporation, 109, 113
Beck, Warren A., 20
Bell, Phillip A., 12, 13, 14, 15, 20, 21
Berkeley:
  California, 17
  Camp Ashby, 108
  campaign for fair employment, 78-79
  Chamber of Commerce, 98
  City Council, 77, 98, 99
  1880 census, 20
  Fair Housing Law, 151
  housing project, 99
  Manufacturer's Association, 99
  police force, 59
  public school integration, 79
  See University of California, Berkeley
Berkeley Gazette, 77
Berkley, Tom, 60
Berwanger, Eugene, 5, 24n.5
Bethune, Mary McLeod, 62, 72
Birth of a Nation, 38, 39, 59
Bishop G.W. Clinton Club, 37
Black Billy Sunday, 60
Black Cross Nursing Corps, 56, 57
Black Independent Club. *See* Equal Rights League

Index

Boilermakers' Union, 106, 107
Bonus Army March, 103
Borthwick, J.D., 5
Bowen, William, 20
Brady, Tom, 45
Brent, Arthur Lowell, 44
Bridges, Harry, 74, 88n.70
Broussard, Albert S., 123n.1
Brotherhood of Sleeping Car Porters, 61, 66, 67-68, 86n.38, 101, 102, 105, 111
Brown, Charlotte, 20
Brown, Edmund G. (Pat), 142, 145, 146
Brown, John, 6
Brown, Richard Maxwell, 52n.31, 155
Brown, Tilghman, 37
Brown vs. Omnibus Railroad Company, 20
Bulldozing, 31, 50n.1
Bulletin, 12, 20
Bunch III, Lonnie G., 27n.38
Bureau of Investigation, 43, 44, 45, 46, 52n.39-43, 53n.47, 56, 83n.3, 114
Burnett, Peter, 6, 7, 19
Burns, Hugh, 142
Butler, Edward, 112, 113
Butler, Walter, 38-39
Butler, William P., 81
Byrne family, 17

Cagayan Mountains, 32
California:
  Assembly, 12, 71
  Assembly Bill 807, 138
  Assembly Bill 1240, 147, 151
  blacks in, 3
  Chamber of Commerce, 151
  Chinese in, 14, 15, 16, 17
  Constitutional Convention, 1849, 4
  Criminal Practices Act, Section 14, 7
  Dream, 4, 9, 10, 49, 55, 64, 91, 108, 152, 155
  Fair Employment Practices Committee, 139, 140
  Fair Employment Practices Commission, 143
  Federation of Labor, 42, 152
  Gold Rush, 5
  Homestead laws, 10
  Legislature, 11, 16, 70
  National Guard, 138
  National Youth Administration, 72
  Relief Administration, 70
  residency requirement, 93
  Senate, 8, 12
  Senate Committee on Military and Veterans Affairs, 138
  Spanish, 4
  State Employment Service, 108
  Supreme Court on union auxiliaries, 113-114
  See University of California, Berkeley
  war in, 46

California Council of Negro
   Women, 144
California Real Estate
   Association, 145, 151
California State Association
   of Colored Women's
   Clubs, 62
California Voice, 55, 56, 57,
   58, 60, 61, 80
Californian, San Francisco, 3
Camp Funston, Ka, 48
Campbell Village, 81, 97,
   144
Caraway, Thaddeus H., 46
Carey, Edward J., 136
Carroll, Charles, 38
Central Pacific Railroad, 16,
   20, 31
Chase, Gordon, 7
Chatham, Canada, 6
Chicago Defender, 44
Chicago effect, 91
Chicago Tribune, 43
Chicago Whip, 69
Chile, 4
Chinese:
   immigration to California,
      16, 17
   population, 28n.59
   suffrage, 18
City Railway Cars, 20
Civil Rights Act, 1866, 15
Citizen's Employment
   Council, 78
Civil Service:
   employment for African
      Americans, 19
   training, 72

Claremont Improvement
   Club, 100
Clark, George, 87n.49
Coakley, James F., 119
Cobb, General, 13
Colbert, Robert E., 93,
   123n.9
Coleman, Edward L., 92,
   118, 123n.5-6
Colley, Nat, 140
Color Question, 48
Colton, Walter, 25n.8
Commodore, 8
Commonwealth Progressive
   Party, 76
Congress on Racial Equality
   (CORE), 146, 147
Conscription Act, 45
Contra Costa area, 21
Convention for the
   Improvement of Free
   People of Color, 4
Cooper, William P., 95
Coppin, Fanny Jackson, 36
Cordonices Village, 99, 145
Cowles, Robert, 7
Coxhead, Ernest, 41
Coy, Wayne, 103
Crawford, Matt, 129
Crisis, The, 44, 47, 48
Cristobal, Juan, 4
Crouchett, Lawrence P.,
   27n.38, 58, 83n.4, 123n.1
Crum, Bartley, 112
Crummer, J.E., 56
Crusader, The, 44
Culinary Workers
   International, 76

Daly, Elbert A., 129

Index

Daniels, Douglas Henry, 24n.2, 108, 123n.10
Davie, Mayor, 40
Defense industries, 91
De Fremery Park Hospitality House, 115-116
Dellums, C.L.:
  Correspondence and Papers, 127n.75
  in General Strike, 1934, 74
  in NAACP, 61, 71, 133, 135
  launching Liberty ship, 107
  leads housing protest, 80-81, 100
  March on Washington Movement, 100, 102, 106
  migrates to California, 65
  on Alameda County Central Labor Council, 76
  on bail for prisoners at county jail, 135
  on California Fair Employment Practices Commission, 139-140
  opposes 1946 Fair Employment Practices Bill, 136
  oral history, 72, 139
  organizer for the Brotherhood of Sleeping Car Porters, 66-67
  opposes Negro section of NYA, 72
  remembers Tulsa riots, 60
  serves on East Bay Draft Board, 114-115
  supports Fair Employment Practices Bill, 136, 139, 141-142
  supports Fair Employment Practices Commission, 114
  supports Joseph James in Marinship, 111, 113
  vice-president for Brotherhood of Sleeping Car Porters, 68
  works for the Pullman Company, 66
  works with Harry Bridges, 74-75
Dellums, William, 60
Delta Sigma Theta Sorority, 58
Democratic Party, 19
Dennis, J.A., 37-38
Depression, Great, 70
Despol, John, 140
Dickson, Dr., 79
Dining Car Cooks and Waiters Union, 33, 106, 108
Discrimination:
  economic, 131
  National Guard, 137-138
  residential, 96-98, 99-100, 145
  separate but equal all-black union locals, 114
  workplace, 104, 105
Dixon, Thomas, 38
Doak, Thomas, 4
Downey, Sheridan, 72
Douglas, Helen Gahagan, 72
Douglass, Frederick, 26n.21

Draft evasion:
  slacker raids, 46
DuBois, W.E.B., 47, 61
Dwinelle, John W., 15-16

Early, Stephen, 100-101, 103
East Bay Boilermakers
  Local 681, 113
East Bay Women's Welfare
  Club, 78, 79, 115
El Caney, 31-32
El Dorado, 3, 5, 8, 92
Elevator, 9, 13, 153
Elier, Paul, 73
Emancipator, The, 44
End Poverty in California
  (EPIC), 77
Ensenada, 45
Equal Rights League, 15, 19
Espionage Act, 46
Estell, James, 25n.13
Ethiopian, 56
Evening Journal, 12
Examiner, San Francisco, 16, 17
Executive Order 8802, 104, 105, 106, 107, 108

Fair Employment Practices
  Act, 104, 121
Fair Employment Practices
  Bill, 135-136, 139
Fair Employment Practices
  Commission, 105, 106, 108, 112-113, 133, 134
Fair Housing Act, 147, 154
Fallon, Father, 45
Fanny Jackson Coppin Club, 36, 62

Fanny Wall Children's
  Home, 36
Federal Bureau of
  Investigation. *See*
  Bureau of Investigation
Federal Housing
  Administration, 80
Federal Theatre Project, 78
Federation of Women's
  Clubs:
  California State
    Convention, 62
  meeting in Oakland, 1926, 62
  Northern, 36
Fifteenth Amendment, 18, 19, 39
Fillmore district, 110, 126n.57
Finney, Senator, 16
Flory, Ishmael, 76
Forbes, Jack D., 24n.2
Ford, John Anson, 143
Forrestal, James V., 119, 120, 121
Fourteenth Amendement, 15, 17
France, Edward E., 17, 18
Franchise League, 7
Franciscans, 3
Frazier, Rosa, 33
Free Black Communities:
  New Bedford, Ma, 5, 25n.18
  New York City, 5
Fugitive Slave Law, 9, 17

Gaines, E.L., 56
Garrison, William Lloyd, 26n.21

Index

Garvey, Marcus, 44-45, 56, 57, 58, 83n.3
General Strike, 1934, 73-75, 77
George Washington Carver, 107
Germany, 45, 48
Gesell Committee, 138, 149n.23
Gibson, Luther, 142, 145
Gilbert, Edward, 4
Gilman, Thomas, 5
Golden Gate steamship, 10
Golden State Mutual Insurance Company, 64
Gordon, Walter A., 58, 121
Goss, Nelson, 116, 118-119, 127n.80
Grace Line, 73, 75
Grandfather Clause, 39, 64
Granger, Lester, 121
Green, Arthur, 99
Green, William, 68, 113
Guinn v. United States, 39
Gwin, Jr., William M., 28n.59

Haggerty, C.J., 140
Haight, Henry H., 18
Haight, Raymond L., 76-77
Hampton Quartet, 42
Harper's Ferry, 6
Hawkins, Augustus F., 71, 72, 88n.58, 135, 136, 139, 140, 143
Herald and Mirror, 12
Henderson, J.C., 120
Herndon, Angelo, 75, 89n.75
Highland Training Hospital, 71

Hill, T. Arnold, 100, 101
Hillman, Sidney, 103, 104
Hines, Albert L., 135
Hitler, Adolf, 116
Home for Aged and Infirm Colored People, 33
Homestead Question, 11, 13
Hoover, J. Edgar, 44
Horne, Lena, 107
Hoskins, J.R., 107
Howser, Fred N., 138
Hudson, Oscar, 47
Huggins, Nathan, 84n.12, 154
Hurley, Edgar S., 137

Iba, Philippines, 32
Independent Sunday School Club, 36
Industrial Association of San Francisco, 73
International Association of Machinists, 76
International Brotherhood of Boilermakers and Iron Shipbuilders and Helpers of America: auxiliaries, 76, 106-107, 110, 112
International Longshoremen's and Warehousemen's Union (ILWU), 75
International Longshoremen's Association (ILA): Bridges, Harry, 74, 75
General Strike, 1934, 73
position on crew of *Santa Rosa*, 75

International Seamen's
  Union, 75

Jackson, Louie, 40
Jackson, William Albert, 57
James, Joseph, 108, 110,
  111, 112, 113, 114, 120
James v. Marinship, 108,
  110-113
Japan, 44, 45, 52n.43
Japantown, 110
Japanese All-Stars of
  Alameda, 64
Jefferson, Thomas Lion, 44
Johnson, Clarence, 106
Johnson, H.T.S., 60-61
Johnson, Hugh S., 88n70
Johnson, Lyndon Baines,
  138
Johnston, George, 7
Jones, James Wormley, 44
Jones, O.E., 37
Jourdan, Spencer, 107

Kaiser, Henry J., 92
  integration of Kaiser
  industries, 93
  shipyards, 94, 106, 107,
  109, 113
Keeton Chorus, 78
Kelley, Florence, 61
Kenny, Robert, 112
Key Route Transit System,
  132-134
Kilpatrick, Vernon, 139
Kingman, Harry L., 133-134
Knox, Frank, 100, 104, 119
Knudsen, William, 103, 104

La Guardia, Fiorello, 103-
  104
Labor's Non-Partisan
  League, 81
Ladies Ministerial Aid
  Society, 22
Land, Emory S., 111
Lapp, Rudolph M., 24n.2
Las Guasimas, 31
Lawton, General, 32
League of Women Voters,
  81
Lee, Archy, 7-8
Lenier, O'Hara, 72
Lewis, Irma, 120
Liberator, 5
Liberty Ships, 107
Linden Center, YWCA, 63
Limerick, Patricia Nelson,
  14, 24n.1
Littlejohn, J.E., 45
Lockett, Royal, 19
Lockwood Housing Project,
  81
Long Hairs. *See* Republican
  Unionists
Los Angeles Merchants and
  Manufacturers
  Association, 141
Louis, Joe, 132
Loving, Walter, 42
Luckenbach Steamship
  Company, 65, 73
Lunar Visitor, 12
Lundeberg, Harry, 132
Lynching, 43, 45, 48

McAteer, Gene, 142
McBeth, Hugh M.
  (MacBeth), 45

Index

McClane, Reverend, 45
McCollister, Richard H., 137
McCurry, Lucie, 132
McDougal, 6
McEntire, Davis, 134-135
MacGowan, Charles, 113
McPherson, J. Gordon, 60
Manhattan Club, 10
March on Washington:
   Committee, 102, 105, 136
   Movement, 100, 101, 102, 105, 125n.36
Mare Island, 42, 52n.30
Marin Citizen, 109
Marin City, 109
Marine Cooks and Stewards Union, 33
Marin-er, 110-111
Marinship, 92, 108-109, 111, 112, 113, 114
Marshall, Thurgood, 112, 120
Marysville, 10
Mason, Lena, 37
Masons:
   Negro Masonic Lodge, 23, 65
   Prince Hall Masons, 66, 85n.34
Maynes, George R., 45
Measure C, 151
Merriam, Frank, 76, 77
Messenger, The, 44, 46, 49, 65
Methodist Church:
   Beebe Memorial A.M.E. Temple, 136-137
   Bethel A.M.E. Church, 37
   colored, in Sacramento, 8

   Cooper A.M.E. Zion Church, 12, 22, 36
   15th Street First A.M.E. Church, 37, 62
   Parks Chapel Church, 61, 67
   Shiloh A.M.E. Church, Oakland, 15, 22
Mexico, 3, 4, 45, 46, 52n.43
Migration, Great, 44
Miller, George, 142
Miller, Nathan Henry, 71
Mirror of the Times, 9
Mission, Santa Barbara, 4
Molitar, Tony, 50n.5
Mooney, Tom, 75, 89n.76
Morning Call, 12, 13
Moore, Dad, 86n.46
Moore, John J., 12
Moore, Ruth P., 63-64
Moore, Shirley Ann, 156n.8
Moore Shipyards, 43, 92, 106
Myrdal, Gunnar, 104

Nash, Jay B., 62
NAACP, 39, 44, 51n.22, 56, 59, 61, 62, 70, 80, 110, 112, 120, 130-131, 132, 133, 135, 139, 151
National Association of Colored Women (NACW), 62
National Labor Relations Board, 110
National Maritime Union:
   Porkchops, 131
National Youth Administration (NYA), 72, 104

Navy, Spanish, 3
Negro Business League, 35, 56
Negro Educational Council of the East Bay, 82
Negro Testimony Bill. *See* Perkins Bill
Negroes in the News, 82
New Deal:
  Agricultural Adjustment Act, 76
  Federal Housing Authority, 80
  Federal Theatre Project, 78
  public works projects, 71, 72
New Granada, Panama, 7
New Leadership Clubs, 76
Newby, William H., 23
Niblack, Rear Adm. A.P., 44
Nichols, Galen, 46
Nigger Bar, 5, 24n.7
Northern Federation Home and Day Nursery, 36

O'Dwyer, Msgr., 140
Oakland:
  Acorn project, 144
  automobile plants, 43
  Athens of the West, 21, 37
  Board of Education, 27n.46
  Board of Supervisors, 133
  Brooklyn public school, 15
  Chamber of Commerce, 42
  Citizens' Committee for Urban Renewal, 144
  City Council, 39, 47, 80, 144
  Civil Service, 19, 40
  County Jail, 63
  De Fremery Park Hospitality House, 115-116
  Equal Rights League, 19
  Fifteenth Assembly District, 77
  Fire Department, 134
  housing, 48, 80-81
  Housing Authority, 80-81
  League of Women Voters, 81
  McDonough Theater, 38
  NAACP chapter, 38, 39, 59, 61, 62
  pier, 50n.8
  Playground Dept., 62
  population
    in 1900, 31
    in 1910, 31
    in 1920, 31
  public school, 13, 15
  Sheriff's Department, 63
  terminus for Central Pacific, 20
  Thirteenth Assembly District, 77
  transportation center, 33-34
  UNIA chapter, 55, 58
  Women's Club, 36, 62
Oakland Colored Giants, 64
Oakland Daily Tribune:
  Delilah Beasley's column, 57
  Knowland family 57
Oakland Independent, 69, 70

Index

Oakland Observer, 130
Oakland Sunshine, 34, 42, 56
Oakland Tribune, 38, 94, 141
Oberlin College, 36
Omnibus Railroad, 20
O.N.I., *See* U.S. Office of Naval Intelligence
Order of Odd Fellows, 37
Osborne, Alice, 59
Osterhaus, Hugo S., 119

Pacific Appeal, 9, 10, 12, 13, 20, 32, 35, 55, 153
Pacific Coast Appeal, 34, 36, 38
Pacific Coast Maritime Federation, 75
Pacific Coast Real Estate and Employment Company of Oakland, 34
Pacific Steamship Company, 65
Palmer, A. Mitchell, 44
Panama Pacific International Exposition, 1915:
  boosterism, 41
  Palace of Fine Arts, 42
  Tower of Jewels, 41
Parchester Village, 145
Patterson, Robert, 100, 104
Pearl Harbor, 106
People's World, 132
Peralta Housing Project, 81
Perkins, Frances, 103
Perkins Bill, 12-13
Perluss, Irving H., 152
Pershing, John J., 46
Peru, 4
Philadelphia, 4

Philippine-American War, 32
Philippines, 32
Philomath Club, 35
Pittman, Tarea Hall, 51n.15, 59:
  acting director of West Coast Regional NAACP, 92
  president of the California State Association of Colored Women's Clubs, 62
  promoted women's maximum security prison at Tehachapi, 63
  recalls segregation of Bay Area jails, 135
  supports California FEP Bill, 142, 149n.33, 150n.35
  works for Richmond Travelers Aid Society, USO, 93, 94
Pleasant, Mary Ellen (Mammy), 6, 25n.12
Poole, W.B., 45
Port Chicago:
  Bob Anderson's documentary film, 127n.87
  E.A. Bryan, 117, 118
  explosion, 117-118
  loading of ammunition, 117
  mutiny, 116, 117-118
  mutiny trial, 119-121
  Quinalt Victory, 117, 118
  U.S. Naval Installation, 116

Port Chicago (cont'd)
  Vogel, Peter, 127n.87
Porter, Kenneth Wiggins, 24n.2
Populist Party, 43
Powers, Robert B., 135
Proposition 14, 151-152
Pullman Club, 64
Pullman Company, 20, 31, 40, 57, 66-67, 68-69, 86n.37-41
Purnell, William W., 32
Purnell, Z.J., 19

Rabb, Earl, 140
Race, Riots:
  Atlanta, Ga, 1906, 38
  Detroit, Mi, 1943, 111
  Houston, Tx, 1917, 46, 47, 53n.49-52
  Los Angeles, 1943, 111
  Springfield, Il, 1908, 38
  Tulsa, Ok, 1920-21, 60
Railroad Porters Club, 36
Railway Labor Act, 67
Randolph, A. Philip, 44, 65, 67, 68, 86n.45, 100-102, 103, 104, 105, 133, 136
Rattigan, Joseph A., 146
Rauh, Joseph L., 104
Red Scare of 1919, 44
Redcaps of Oakland, 33
Regan, Bruce V., 146
Republican Unionists, 16
Ressner, Herbert, 112
Richmond, CA, 33, 43
  Chamber of Commerce, 96
  City Council, 94-95, 96
  Dormitory "O" fire, 95
  Fair Employment Practices survey, 140-141
  Housing Authority, 96
  Kaiser Shipyards, 92
  launching of Liberty ships, 107-108
  Police Department, 134-135
  public housing, 94, 95, 96
  Recreational Department, 107
  Richmond Housing Authority, 95
  Standard Oil Refinery, 43
  Travelers Aid Society, 93, 94
  Wall's Addition, 80, 90n.92
  wartime transformation, 94
Right to Testimony, 10, 11
Ripoll, Father, 4
Roche, Michael, 112
Rolph, James, 76
Roosevelt, Eleanor, 103-104
Roosevelt, Franklin D., 71, 77, 100-101, 104, 112, 119
Rosenberg, Anna, 104
Ross, Malcolm, 113
Rossi, Mayor, 73
Roswell, Irving P., 45
Roybal, Ed, 140
Rumford, William Byron:
  appointed to Berkeley Emergency Housing Commision, 136
  appointed to California Housing Commission, 136

Index

Rumford (cont'd)
  at University of California, 59-60
  campaign for State Assembly, 60
  elected to California Legislature, 135, 137
  fails exam for California State Board of Pharmacy investigator, 132
  introduces Assembly Bill 32, 139
  introduces fair housing bill, 145, 146
  on Fair Housing Act, 151
  on Proposition 14, 151
  spokesperson for minority rights, 137
  student activism, 60
  supports California FEP, 136, 139
Ryan, Joseph P., 74

Sacramento, 7, 10
Sacramento Market, 78-79
St. Sure, Paul, 112
San Francisco:
  Californian, 3
  Committee Against Segregation and Discrimination, 110, 111, 112
  earthquake of 1906, 34, 40
  Hospitality House and Dance Hall, 115
  Labor Council, 42, 43
  See Panama Pacific International Exposition
  Presidio, 42

San Francisco *Examiner*, 111
San Francisco News, 77
San Jose, 6
San Juan Hill, 32
San Miguel, General, 32
San Quentin, 75
San Rafael *Daily Independent*, 111
Sanderson, Jeremiah B., 13, 19
Sanderson, Mary, 13
Sandwich Islands, 4
Santa Fe:
  Ferryboats, 34
  Railroad, 33
  Tract, 48
Santiago, Felipe, 4
Sarber, J. Delbert, 98
Savage, William Sherman, 24n.2
Saxton, Alexander, 15
Scharrenberg, Paul, 42
Schmitz, John G., 151
Schnitzer, Robert C., 78
Seaman:
  African-American, 3
  Jack Tars, 4
Selective Service Act, 48
Selvage, Hudson, 46
Seventy-six Clubs, 76
Shape-up, 73, 74, 75, 88n.67
Sheffield Village, 80
Shelton, Julia Ann, 33
Shorey, Capt. William T., 33, 35, 50n.7
Short Hairs, 16
Shufeldt, Robert, 38
Sidney, New South Wales, 4
Sinclair, Upton, 77

Slavery:
  in California, 4, 5
  in Galveston, Texas, 14
Small, Eugene, 111
Small, Joseph, 116
Smith, Alonzo, 104
Smith, Kenneth, 134
Smith, Mike, 72
Snape, John, 60
Social Darwinism, 21, 41, 51n26
Sonora, Mexico, 7
Southern Pacific Railroad, 31, 65
Spanish-American War, 31
Spear, Allan, 91
Spooner, Bill, 68
Staats, Redmond C., 99
Stallinger, Preston, 111
Stanford, Gov. Leland, 13
Starr, Kevin, 21, 24n.1
State Convention of Colored Citizens:
  Executive Committee, 8, 10, 11
  Address, 1859, 9, 11, 26n.24
  First State Convention, 9
  in 1855, 8
  in 1865, 18
  in 1873, 18
  Procedings of, 26n.20
Stephens, Virginia, 41
Stimson, Henry, 103, 104
Stockton:
  Statewide black educational conference, 15
Stovall, C.A., 7
Strothoff, Charles, 96

Sutphin, Dudley V., 47
Sweet's Ballroom, 67

Tanner, Henry O., 42
Taylor, Quintard, 104
Tehachapi prison, 63
Thirteenth Amendment, 15, 17
Thorn-Scott, Elizabeth, 13
Tillman, Robert, 47
Tillman court-martial, 47
Tippton, William, 35
Titus, Earl E., 44
Todd-California Shipyard, 92, 95, 118
Tompkins, E. Berkeley, 50n.7
Trade unionists, 105
Treasure Island:
  International Exposition, 78
  Naval Base, 119
Swing Mikado, 110
Troy, Theodore, 45
Truman War Investigation Committee, 99

Unemployment Insurance Administration, 70
Union Party, 16
United Negro Improvement Association:
  Black Cross Nursing Corps, 56, 57
  Digest, 56
  Oakland chapter, 55-56
  Papers, 83n.3
  Women's Auxiliary, 56
United Negro Labor Committee, 107

Index 195

United States:
 Army Intelligence, 43
 Cavalry, Ninth, 46
 Cavalry, Tenth, 46
 Commission on Civil
  Rights, 92
 Department of Labor, 45
 Department of Justice, 43,
  44, 54n.55, 56, 83n.3
 Department of State, 43
 Employment Service, 104
 General Intelligence
  Division, 44
 Housing Authority, 95, 96,
  98, 99
 Infantry, 24th, 42, 46,
  53n.49
 Infantry, 25th, 32
 Maritime Commission,
  109, 111
 Navy policies, 121
 Office of Naval
  Intelligence, 43, 44
 Postal Deparment, 43, 46
 Supreme Court, 64, 75
University of California,
 Berkeley, 57, 58, 59
Unruh, Jesse, 143, 146
Urban League, 87n.57,
 130-131, 132, 134

Vallejo Navy Yard, 43
Van Ostrand, Randolph, 141
Vancouver Island, 7
Veltmann, Gerald E., 120
Venderlip, L.C., 141

War Manpower
 Commission, 104
Warner, Stuart, 83

Warner Brothers Studies, 82
Warren, Earl:
 cross-filing in 1946, 136
 District Attorney,
  Alameda, 71
 does not endorse
  California FEP, 136
 early career, 59
 in gubernatorial campaign,
  1934, 76
 meets Legislator Rumford,
  137
 on FEP Bill, 142
 Oral History Project,
  84n.10
Watkins, John, 130
Washington, Booker T.:
 accommodationist
  doctrine, 19, 35
 caricature in *Crisis*, 49
 Negro Business League,
  35
Webster, Milton P., 86n46,
 101, 106
Western American, 54
White, Walter, 100, 101,
 103, 104
Wilberforce University, 37
Wilds, John, 19
Williams, Aubrey, 104
Williams, David A., 20
Williams, James, 133
Williams, Tobe, 37
Wilson, Hannah, 17
Wilson, Peter, 17
Winnacker, Martha Kendall,
 27n.38
Wollenberg, Charles,
 126n54-55

Women's Clubs. *See also*
  Federation of Women's
  Clubs; California State
Women's Clubs (cont'd)
  Association of Colored
  Women's Clubs
Woodson, Carter G., 50n.1
Works Progress
  Administration, 71, 78
World War I, 34, 43, 44, 45,
  48, 49, 52n.34, 55, 56,
  59, 70, 115
World War II, 75, 82, 91,
  92, 93, 94, 97, 100, 106,
  108, 110, 114-115, 116,
  121, 129, 144, 154
Wright, Carleton H., 119,
  120
Wysinger vs. Crookshank, 16

Yates, William H., 8, 9-10
Young Men's Christian
  Association, 63, 71
Young Women's Christian
  Association, Linden
  Branch:
  college football
  tournament, 64
  funding drive, 64
  Ruth Moore, 63